A SPIRIT WORK PRIMER

A SPIRIT WORK PRIMER

A Beginner's Guide to Streamlined Spirit Work

NAAG LOKI SHIVANATH

Crossed Crow Books

Foreword to the new edition by Chris Allaun.
Foreword to the original edition by Charles L. McBride.
Cover design and interior illustrations by Wycke Malliway.
Published by Crossed Crow Books. Chicago, IL

Second Edition, 2022.

Library of Congress Control Number: 2022931831
ISBN 979-8-9856281-0-4

Crossed Crow Books
1407 W Morse Ave
Chicago, IL 60626
www.CrossedCrowBooks.com

Printed in the United States of America.

This work is dedicated to all of those many people who have supported me in my path, practice, and art, to my first edition editor, S. D. Greene, to the folks over at Crossed Crow Books for enjoying this work so much that they decided to offer me a deal on a new edition, and especially to my loving wife, Samantha, who has put up with my obsessive need to write when I should probably be folding clothes.

CONTENTS

Dedication   v
Foreword To The New Edition   ix
Foreword To The Original Edition   xv
Introduction To The New Edition   xix
Introduction To The Original Edition   xxi

I   The Basics of Spirit Work   1

II   The Nature of Offerings   13

III   Spirit Senses   25

IV   Magickal Invocation   33

V   Magickal Evocation   43

VI   The Nature of Spiritual Pacts   53

VII   Spirit Possession   75

VIII   Familiar Spirits   87

IX   Spirit Keeping   95

X   Isolated Spirits   101

XI   Created Spirits   107

XII Spirit Houses   115

XIII Spiritual Self-Defense and Cleanup   123

XIV Grimoire of the Thorn   135

Parting Words   153
Glossary Of Terms   155
Glossary Of Spirits   161
References & Suggested Reading   171

FOREWORD TO THE NEW EDITION

This is the book I wish I had when I first began learning spirit conjuration. Naag does a great job of taking the reader through various aspects of advanced spirit work in a way that is practical and easy to understand. I have personally found that many books on spirit conjuration tend to be written in such a grandiose way, and the student of the occult who is serious about pursuing this aspect of magick is left feeling more confused than anything. My first exposure to spirit work came many moons ago when I was newly initiated into an aspect of traditional witchcraft while simultaneously undertaking a course of study with the OTO. You see, the bread and butter, so to speak, of these two traditions is communion with the spirit world. It was taught that any magician or Witch worth the broom could summon the spirits and get them to perform great works of magick for you. In one instance, the Witch may find themselves called to conjure forth a familiar spirit while, comparatively, a magician may find themselves invoking any number of gods or goddesses and entering into compacts with these forces for the purposes of gaining success in certain endeavors, winning love, or even restoring health.

There are old books, grimoires, and manuscripts that talk about summoning demons and other powerful spirits, but oftentimes these ancient tomes did not tell you how these beings were to be summoned. (And the few that did tell you had instructions that were so complicated that very few would be able to attempt them in the modern day.) My teachers at the time suggested that the magician already knew how to perform these great works of magick and that the books were only there to remind you of what you were doing. In essence, the books were a barebones outline that was meant only for the initiated and the students already trained in the arts of magick.

As you can probably imagine, this would have been very disheartening and incredibly frustrating. On top of that, many students learning this type of magick would often throw caution to the wind and do the best they could with these old books using what little training they had. The outcome? Well, either nothing happened or the student would have inadvertently opened a portal from goddess knows where and summon a spirit that they knew very little about. This could have led to many problems then, as well as in the modern day, as there have been many a night where I had been called upon to help someone banish some wayward spirit. Luckily, I was trained in advanced psychic self-defense and spirit work so I was often called to a colleague's home to help them put back whatever it was that they summoned that would not go back home. I could tell you a story or two, believe me!

I also knew of many magicians and witches who worked with several kinds of spirits and kept them in jars, cauldrons, statues, and mojo bags. Each spirit had a different job and would perform great works of magick for the magician. As a young witch, I always thought this was the coolest thing, but found myself getting more and more frustrated when I would ask how these witches would have accomplished this. "Just do it" or "when the time is right you will learn" were the two common answers, both of which led me to believe that they didn't actually know how to teach these techniques, or they were simply gatekeeping.

I always felt that magicians who didn't take the time to actually sit down and teach students spirit conjuration were keeping the power to themselves. However, to be fair, in my journey of traditional witchcraft, I learned that our teachers and mentors are only there to show us how to open the doors into the Otherworld so the Witch could seek out the spirits on their own while teaching themselves the mysteries. So, that's exactly what I did. Over the years I learned through spirit teachers and filled in any blanks with other like-minded witches and ceremonial magicians. I have learned to work with the spirits in such a way that brings so much magick and fulfillment to my path. I spent many years practicing and perfecting my connection to the spirits, and I know that if I had this book when I first began my journey, I would have achieved that connection so much faster.

As I sat down to read this book, the first thing I noticed is that Naag Loki Shivanath teaches in a way that is similar to my approach. He explains things in a clear and concise manner that speaks to both intermediate and advanced practitioners while leaving the path open for beginners to become inspired to continue their magical practice. I am a firm believer in never assuming that the student already knows something. Maybe they do or maybe they don't. Naag helps the student delve deep into their own magical power and pushes them to become better magicians. Even better is that he gently guides the student to push beyond what they already know and helps them connect to the spirits in a powerful way.

There are many things that I love about this book but one of the things that inspires me is his way of explaining how to actually do the work with the spirits rather than leaving it up to the student to make mistakes and figure it out on their own. Naag gives us clear instructions and he demystifies a lot of the traditional lore of spirit conjurations.

I have already mentioned my hate of gatekeeping---it bothers me to no end. There is a difference between teaching advanced magical practices to a student when they are ready so that they don't hurt themselves or others, and not teaching the student these techniques so that they stay a step behind the teacher. (Naturally, this leaves the teacher on a pedestal in the eyes of the student.) There is so much magick in the world, enough for everyone and then some! With this masterful work, Naag kicks gatekeeping to the curb and gives the student the trust that they will take responsibility for their own actions and their own magical work. Naag wonderfully teaches us what real magick and what it is not through each of these carefully crafted techniques. He teaches us how to work with the spirits in such a way that is congruent to each of our magical paths, no matter how different they are.

I was so impressed that this book was written in such a way that it can be found to speak to witches, ceremonial magicians, and those of us who walk an earth-centered path. Many books focus on either witchcraft, ceremonial magick, or shamanism, but this book is written in such a way that the student can incorporate their own unique path and do amazing work with the spirits.

I was also impressed that Naag teaches the student that the most important thing about working with the spirits is establishing a relationship with them. It's rare that an author teaches this. Naag tells us that working with the spirits isn't just powerful words of summoning with a list of demands. The real power behind this work is to research the spirits, understand them to the best of your ability, and connect with them so that they want to help you with your magick verses being coerced or forced to do the magician's bidding. This is where powerful magick happens---when the magician and the spirits are working in conjunction with a common purpose.

If I had this book 25 years ago when I was learning spirit conjurations, invocation, evocation, spirit pacts, and familiar-work it would have been so much easier for me. I am happy to say that this book will teach you almost everything you need to know to work with the spirits in a variety of ways. Like I said before, Naag doesn't shy away from helping the student sink their teeth into the richness of the spirit world. Be ready to walk into a world of magick and great power. The spirits are watching....they are waiting for you to turn the pages of this book and summon them.

-Chris Allaun
Chicago, IL
January 2022

It is the traditional place of introducing an author in tomes such as these by speaking on their vast wisdom, knowledge, and years of experience. As one of Naag Loki Shivanath's best friends and closest companions, first let me say that he is one of the most well-read mystics I have ever met. I have known him for the better part of six years now, and of all the mystics I know, he is one who has always had some experience in any field I've put him to the test on. Moreover, not just experience in a system as having researched it, but more often than not some practical example of his own workings with it could be made available by request. I would recommend his work on this alone but want to go a bit further.

Often it is the place of the foreword to simply list all the accomplishments and fields of study an author has in the arts mystic within our circles. Instead, today I'd rather recount some workings I've witnessed firsthand. As this book has to do with spirit working, I'll be focusing on a retelling of areas concerning that and focusing on things I have myself witnessed. I feel recounting these events speak more for the skill of my friend and spiritual brother than any recounting of the countless systems he has practiced and mastered.

Of the stories I could tell, I think the most impacting and of note would have to be his working with the demon Bune, who is well known in Goetic magick for bringing wealth. A situation had arisen where a family member needed employment and Naag Loki Shivanath moved into action. After applications of traditional oils and methods like that found wanting, he stepped up his game into the arts of spirit evocation. I was there for this, so I can attest to the truth and validity of this story.

He prepared his tools, began his research to make certain he missed nothing, and within a few hours was ready to begin. His ritual was not an overly complex one, and I won't recount all of it as you will be learning his methods soon enough, though I will say it covered everything of importance and ended with him placing the seal of Bune onto his own chest to finalize the pact. This part is not the fantastic part, as all manner of practitioners have in the past placed seals upon their body. What is of importance in magick is manifestation. Within a day a call was received from this family member; not only had they got the job they were interested in but the call from their interviewer was days early!

Likewise, this manifestation led to interesting results, which Shivanath was prepared to deal with. A few marks appeared on his body at random intervals and as I was staying with him at the time, I had the opportunity to witness his knowledge in action as he deftly was able to hold the demon to the pact. A lesser mystic would have panicked at this, but for one of his experience this was simply another day in the arts. He knew the proper cleansing, proper shielding, and proper offering to place the demon back into compliance and on good terms with him. Likewise, he completed his part of the pact work once the job was secured and stable and no negative repercussions came from the working.

It was like watching a great composer work his art with a world-class orchestra as he handled the events around the evocation, pact-making, and fulfillment of the pact. I bring this example up because it is a good and prime example of his skill brought into action. Not only was this a practical example of spirit working, but it was also an example of how vital having the right knowledge was. While this might have intimidated other practitioners, Shivanath was never deterred from his course and treated the entirety of these events as something he was familiar with. Moreover though, the practicality of this example of his skill is what I want to bring to mind. In countless books on the subject, we hear about how a demon manifested in a circle, or spoke to someone. Even in this case we have the marks left behind. However, many times what we don't see is the practical part of this. The job that was won, the life that was saved, or the marriage reconciled by the work of the practitioner. This is the meat of mystical work, the important part of doing magick.

Looking back on such occurrences I have had the fortune of being there to witness with Shivanath in person, I should retell one more. I myself, while a skilled practitioner of the arts, am what we tend to call energy dense. This means that I have to purposefully let my guard down to sense, feel, or work with spirits. It also means I am not one often susceptible to the influence of their power. On the advisement of another fellow practitioner, Naag Loki Shivanath obtained a particular grimoire, which we do not have the permission to mention the name of here. In working with that text, he decided it was now proper to evoke a spirit from it and asked that I sit outside the circle to both observe and act, just in case extra help was needed. I came prepared with a number of tools and talismans I rarely rely on as there is rarely the need. As I sat watching this evocation, the spirit responded, changing the pitch of the fire and even putting the flame and incenses out when it was commanded to leave. Moreover, I FELT the energy, even with all of my gear. The purpose of recounting this, though, is that it is the skill of the mystic, not simply the power of the spirit called, that brings forth such manifestation. While I have witnessed a number of evocations, the mark of a good evocation, having made contact with a spirit, is that some manifestation occurs in the moment. This was a prime example of such a manifestation.

I could, of course, go into each of Shivanath's many manifestations using his spirit practices, but instead I should hit on the practicality. Shivanath is not a man bound by unnecessary clutter that many of his contemporaries have holding them down. While he is highly versed in the past, he has a keen mind that pulls out the unnecessary and the distracting. He instead focuses on the application and process to achieve manifestation. It is because of this I am proud to introduce his work to you here.

You picked up this book to learn about working with spirits, but moreover you are looking to manifest. Without manifestation, all magick is pointless and simply an exercise in self appeasement. Recognizing that you have chosen one of the true experts in manifestation to show you the ways of spirit working, my advice is to read this text over many times, make notes as you would with a textbook, compare what you find in it against other more classical texts, and you will see clearly that Naag Loki Shivanath has boiled down the formula of manifestation through working with spirits into a method that is both easily understood and immensely practical.

-Charles L. McBride
Norse Shaman and Sorcerer
December 2016

INTRODUCTION TO THE NEW EDITION

Five years ago, I set out to write what I considered to be a groundbreaking book on one of the most talked-about yet most mysterious aspects of the mystical arts. And then, as soon as I published it, the imposter syndrome set in. Was I a fake? Did I just spit a bunch of words out to have a book to my name? But then, the reviews started rolling in. This book helped revolutionize the art of working with spirits for so many people that I was overwhelmed. I knew I had done a good thing.

In the time that has elapsed, I have looked back at this work again and again, answered questions about it, made clarifications to it, and wondered what I would do differently. Now, I have that opportunity. This new edition will cover some of the more common things I'm asked about, such as spirit keeping and protection, and will expand on some things that I've clarified over the years. I've also added in some practical application exercises so that you can get the most out of your work here. Hopefully, the changes we've made to this edition will make this into what I had always hoped it would be.

I've also taken the liberty of adding a small section that was always intended to be expanded upon and made into a second volume, a sort of spiritual successor to this work, but I never took the time to do so. So, in the pages that follow, I will hopefully make this work worth the time to read for the first time, and for those of you who read the first edition, I hope this makes the second edition worth your time to take in.

INTRODUCTION TO THE ORIGINAL EDITION

When I set out to create this book, I thought to myself that it wouldn't be too hard. After all, I had numerous resources to draw on, hadn't I? Courses I have taken, lessons I have written, and books I have read. And, in a way, I was right. I was able to use much of my old work, but it required extensive editing and reformatting, to the point that it would have almost been easier to write it all from scratch. However, what has been produced is, I believe, my greatest compilation of spirit work to date.

This primer only scratches the surface of the great work, of course, but so does any tome. This particular book is not meant to be the 'end all be all' guide and bible to every movement you should make in the circle or every word that should be spoken, but rather a skeleton, a form that you can fill in with your own practice. This is the method I wish I had had when I began my path.

In any event, this method exists now, and is here for you. I have gathered information from a number of resources and compiled it here for you. Several authors were my inspiration for this work, and their works heavily influenced this book. You will find the works and authors that inspired me in the bibliography at the end of this work. I encourage you to seek out and read these works, as they will fill in what gaps that I may have left.

You will also notice that in my basics section, I mention tools, but I rarely mention them throughout the text. This comes back to my preferred method: Take the bare bones from a work, and fill it in with my own practice. This is what I encourage you to do, as it will help you develop a strong personal practice, and perhaps most importantly, will discourage unnecessary dogma. This has always been my message: forget dogma, keep practical experience, and that is what I give you here.

With that in mind, I want to emphasize something that I bring up frequently in the text: research. Research everything you do with this work, and in magick overall, and make sure you compare everything.. Compare your findings against what I have presented here, and see if your findings are the same as mine, or if they differ. If you find many sources with different information, try it all, and see how well each of them works for you. From this, you can build your own practice using the methods that work best for you, while getting rid of the things that do not. This should, as a result, help you develop a much deeper and more rewarding practice.

And, without further delay, I am pleased to present you with the *Spirit Work Primer*.

CHAPTER I

The Basics of Spirit Work

To properly understand magick, one must realize that, though there are many branches and paths of magick, they all break down into two general categories. The first of these is something I have come to refer to as direct work, which is a term used to refer to magick that involves the creation of oils, powders, talismans, and so on. Direct work often requires the magician to be hands-on with an item and to plant that item on their target. This form of magick is considered *direct work* because, while it may involve prayers, invocations, and other methods of calling on spirits, the bulk of the work relies on the magician *getting their hands dirty* with work, so to speak.

The second form of magick is referred to as spirit work, and this is the focus of this work. Spirit work is magick that involves the evocation, invocation, and otherwise petitioning of the spirits. While many people come to magick with the intent of engaging the spirit world, it must be remembered that spirit work is not necessarily the easiest path of magick. In some cases, it can take many years before one sees even a slight manifestation of a spirit. This book seeks to make the path of spirit work more available to the practitioner, whether they are a beginner or an adept.

In the course of this primer, we will cover things such as evocation, invocation, making offerings, and forming pacts with spirits. This is a highly interactive book, and if the work is done with dedication and focus, the practitioner may realize results occurring with much more frequency. It is my hope that this work will assist you in developing your own methods of working with spirits, as I have never been a believer in following the pages of a book to the letter. It has always been more of my preference to read the book, work at the rituals exactly as written a few times, and then to make the rituals my own and make them more personal. That said, many of the things I have written here come from a standpoint of "to do this, you must do this." Take this as a starting point, a foundation, and expand from there.

While personalizing the rituals and methods of spirit work given here is encouraged, there are a few tools you will need to acquire to work within the framework I have provided. You will need a notebook, a pen, an incense burner, an offering dish, a wand, and a ritual dagger, also called an athame.

The notebook and pen will be used to record your experiences with these spirits, as well as any messages they give to you, and to make notes concerning your own path and practice as it relates to this primer. Your incense burner can be any style, as long as it holds incense. My personal favorite is known as a thurible, and often appears as a small brass dish, usually with a few chains on it so that it may be hung from the wall or from a hook. The offering dish varies from tradition to tradition, but for our purposes a general-use offering dish is preferred. Your personal path will play a large role in the selection of your offering dish, but some ideas are an abalone shell, a brass bowl, a plain white porcelain plate, or a large flat crystal. For your wand, you may purchase one from a trusted supplier, but make sure that the one you select resonates with you. It is often preferred to create your own wand, but if you do not possess the skill required, a purchased wand will work just as well. For the athame, you may go with a traditional choice, such as the double-edged, black-handled dagger, or you may go with something with a bit of flair.. Again, the choice of athame depends largely upon your practice and personal preference.

Each of your tools will have to be consecrated, and many traditions have their own methods for this. However, as this is not a book of tradition, but rather a guideline to working with spirits, I will not give you a drawn-out ceremony. If you do not know an ideal method for consecration, you may use this quick method:

Prepare a basin of water mixed with sea salt. The salt should be dissolved in the water before beginning. Gently wash each of your tools in the salt water, aside from the notebook and pen, and gently dry them with a white cloth. Arrange your tools on a white cloth under a full moon. Allow them to sit under the light of a full moon from sundown to sunup for three nights in a row. After the third night, bring your tools inside and place them on your altar. Hold your hands above the tools, palms facing down, close your eyes, and feel the energy flowing out of your hands and into the tools. As you feel a bond forming between yourself and your instruments, say a few words. These words do not have to be anything specific, nor do they have to be an invocation to any specific power. If you feel this is appropriate, then do so, but otherwise, allow the words to flow from your heart and express your desire to use these tools as implements of magick on your path. When this is done, wrap your tools gently in the white cloth and set them aside. Do not disturb your tools for three days. After three days, unwrap each one of your tools, and place them on your altar. Pick each tool up, one at a time, and feel the bond between you both. These tools will assist you in making magick and calling the spirits. If you come across other items that you wish to use in your practice, you may use this consecration technique for them as well.

Once your tools are consecrated, you are one step closer to being ready to perform magick, however, do not forget the importance of researching what you will be doing, or more specifically, who you will be conjuring. Naturally, every spirit is different and as such, every spirit likes different things, and to try and create a blanket system to work with all spirits would be impossible. This text will give information on several spirits that I have personally worked with, but it is important to do your own research as well. In this respect, the Internet has proven to be a great aid to the aspiring magician. It has also proven to be the Achilles heel of magick in some ways, but that is a discussion for another day. Between the availability of information on the Internet and the number of books on the occult available today, you should have no trouble finding information on almost any spirit you wish to work with.

The exceptions to this rule, of course, are the initiatory traditions that rarely write their information down, or even discuss it amongst outsiders. These traditions include paths such as Vodoun, Santeria, and Palo Mayombe. However, there are plenty of systems available to you that publish information on their spirits and inner workings freely.

When researching a spirit for a ritual, there are a few details that are important to note. The first of these is the origin of that spirit. Origins are important because they give us clues into how a particular culture or tradition perceives certain things. These things, in turn, can give us even deeper insight into the appropriate etiquette needed when working with a particular spirit.

After you have determined the culture of origin, the next thing to look for is the habits and tastes of the spirit you are wanting to work with. Each spirit has its own likes and dislikes, and these can vary greatly, even in the same tradition. This is because many spirits have multiple aspects even under one name. Santa Muerte, for instance, is known for having many different aspects, each of them unique and with its own set of customs. Therefore, you should be aware of the aspect of the spirit you wish to contact, and what that aspect prefers as an offering, as well as what would enrage it.

Once you have identified the proper offerings for the spirit you wish to contact, you should next turn your focus to the traditional methods of calling, serving, and communicating with this spirit. In this respect, we are often forced to improvise a bit. This is most prevalent when looking into the Greek deities. While some information has survived, much of the details surrounding the individual cults of deities has been lost. There is enough fragmented history, however, to get a general idea of what is appropriate.

After learning about the spirit's origin and having determined the appropriate offerings, you'll want to see if there are any seals, alternate names, or known invocations of the spirits you are seeking to work with. When you have compiled this information on the spirit you are attempting to contact, it is time to start making preparations. Gather the items you will need, and prepare your ceremonial area appropriately. The idea is to make the spirit comfortable in your space so that it is more likely to manifest for you. However, we will get into specifics of this in a later chapter.

Once you have completed the research aspect of spirit work, the next phase for any kind of spirit work is the immersion phase. This is the time when you surround yourself with imagery relating to this spirit, and study every detail you can about it. The reason for this is that the law of vibration must be observed. According to the law of vibration, when we wish to draw something to us, we must put out identical vibrations. Immersion is the most effective way to release vibrations that are concurrent with the spirit you wish to contact. Therefore, it is advised that you spend at least thirty days of immersion before beginning spirit work. As you become accustomed to spirit work, and especially as you develop relationships with the spirits you work with frequently, this immersion can become shorter and shorter, until it is no longer necessary for you to make a solid connection.

Another aspect of the immersion cycle is the offering cycle. During this cycle, you will check your research notes on the things that your spirit likes and gather them together to make offerings to the spirit. Offerings can be a very long and detailed ceremony, or they can be a rather quick and efficient ritual. During the immersion phase, however, it is best to take a middle-ground approach. What I mean by this is that while your offering does not have to be an hour-long ceremony, it should be more than placing items on a dish and leaving it on your altar. We will dive into offerings headlong in the next chapter, but for now, you can take a look at this offering ceremony:

A Simple Offering Ceremony

Arrange your temple, altar, or working space and the things that the spirit likes. These can be appropriate colors, metals associated with the spirit, shapes and images that correspond to the spirit, and candles of an appropriate scent and color. Of course, your space can contain more than these things, and it can contain less, but it should contain at least three correspondent settings that the spirit will enjoy. Once your space is prepared for the offering, bring out your offering dish and place your offerings upon it. It is also appropriate to set a special candle for the spirit as an offering, as well as to light incense, but this is up to you and whether or not you wish to make these a part of the offering. These can also be the main offering itself, as some spirits prefer incense or the setting of lights to food, drink, or other offerings. This will depend upon your own discretion, as well as your previous research. Once your offerings have been placed, call the spirit in a manner that is in accordance with its cultural prefer-ence. For instance, if you were making an offering to the Morrigan, you may place upon your dish a glass of dark beer and a dagger to be dedicated to her service. You may also set aside a dragon's blood novena candle as well as dragon's blood incense. When these things are placed, you may light the candle and the incense, and then call her forth with a chant that is of your own making, but that refer-ences her role in the Celtic pantheon as the mistress of magick, and as the goddess of death and war. Specific invocations and evocations of the spirits will be given in a later chapter, but it is best if you form your own calls based upon your research. Spend some time in silent contemplation, seeing, sensing, or otherwise experiencing the presence of the spirit.

As you consistently perform your offering during the immersion phase, you will find yourself being drawn more and more to the spirit you are working with, and you will see the spirit begin to manifest in your life. Using the above example of the Morrigan, you may begin to see crows and ravens appearing to you in groups of threes. This is a clear sign of her presence, and it is one of the ways she communicates with those who are dedicated to her. You will learn to notice these small signs in your life, and to know what it is that they mean for you specifically. There is no set interpretation of these signs, so you will have to trust your intuition.

Aside from offerings, another important aspect of the immersion phase is meditation. This can be done in a variety of ways, which are largely at your discretion. However, some of the best methods are the meditation on the symbol of the spirit and the chanting of the spirit's name as a mantra. Whichever method you prefer, or both if you choose to practice both, perform this meditation at least once a day during your immersion cycle. Like the offering cycle, meditation will bring you into alignment with the spirit you are working with.

An important aspect to remember during the immersion phase is that some spirits do not get along well with others. For instance, you would not want to work with Odin during the same immersion cycle that you were working with Laufey. The wrong combination of spirits can prove dangerous, or perhaps even fatal to the magician. On the other side of this, the right combination of spirits can amplify their abilities greatly. An example of this would be concurrent immersion cycles with both Thor and Odin.

Aside from the immersion phase, one more important thing to remember is that the spirits, like people, have their own personalities, habits, and lives. They are not simply beings from another realm that exists to serve your every wish. This is a vital aspect of spirit work and should not be forgotten. A good analogy for this is that if you were to walk up to a random person on the street and ask for $100, they would likely tell you no. If you were to approach a friend and ask for $100, they may be inclined to loan you the money, but they will expect to be paid back. But if you were to approach your best friend and ask for $100, they would be likely to give you the money, plus extra, and not expect anything in return. This is because of the relationship that the two of you share. Spirits work the same way. You cannot call a spirit for the first time and expect that they will simply manifest your desires as you command them. A relationship needs to be built, and this is the point of the immersion phase. Not only does it bring you into alignment with the spirit, but it also lays the groundwork for a powerful relationship. Bear this in mind when you begin your spirit work, and do not neglect the relationships you build, and your magick will prove very effective.

There are many ways to classify the spirits of the many realms. Typically, these include dualities, such as greater and lesser, light and dark, hot and cold, and isolated and global. There are other ways to classify spirits, but generally speaking, these dualities cover most everything. Let us begin our look at spirit classification with the first pair of classes.

Greater and Lesser Spirits

Greater spirits can be said to be spirits such as the deities, the names of God, which have taken on their own aspects, and even well-known beings such as the demons of the Lesser Key of Solomon, or the archangels. These beings are considered to be greater because they are more potent, and have a further reach, than the lesser spirits. The greater spirits are called upon frequently, and are very well known. This gives them a great deal of influence over our world, because we allow them to, due to their reputation. Lesser spirits, on the other hand, are spirits such as the shades of the dead, spirits of nature, and most created spirits. These spirits are not as well known as the greater spirits and are generally not as powerful. However, these lesser spirits often specialize in one or a few areas, and in these areas their strength can be said to surpass the greater spirits. Lesser spirits are typically called upon for natural magick, such as Celtic and fairy-based magick, as well as for things like necromancy, and even baneful magick. This is due to their areas of specialization, as well as their ease of contact.

Dark and Light Spirits

The next duality we will look at is the duality of dark and light. Of course, light and dark do not equate to good and evil. They are simply elemental classifications. Dark spirits tend to be stern, aggressive, and more prone to violence. Examples of dark spirits include the Morrigan, Lilith, Kali, and many of the shades of the dead. These spirits are considered dark because their nature tends toward darkness, meaning that they are often considered nocturnal, and they can frequently be malicious toward both the magician and their target. This is not to say, however, that they are evil, and in fact, dark spirits can often be the ideal choice for many workings that would be considered positive. Dark spirits are often used for removing obstacles, spiritual growth, and healing past trauma. Light spirits, on the other hand, are typically taken to be more benevolent in nature, calmer, and all around more beneficial. These spirits are often called upon for protection and healing, but they are also often called to deal with enemies. A prime example of this is the archangel Saint Michael, who is called to destroy the forces of darkness coming against the magician. However, as I have said, dark does not equal evil, and light does not equal good. Bear this in mind when considering working with spirits that are dark or light in nature.

Hot and Cold Spirits

Another duality worth looking at is the duality of hot and cold. This distinction often arises in systems such as Vodoun, where spirits are said to be hot or cold depending on how fast they work. The faster a spirit works, the hotter it is said to be, while colder spirits work slower. However, hot spirits tend to work only for a result, rather than the well-being of the magician, while colder spirits tend to work slower precisely because they consider the better good of the magician. Outside of Vodoun, a prime example of this duality exists in the difference between demons and angels. Angels are typically considered to be colder spirits, working slower, but also focusing on the bigger picture, as well as the greater good of the magician. Demons, on the other hand, are typically held to be hotter spirits, but they do not often consider whether or not the result they are working toward will actually benefit the magician in the long run.

Isolated and Global Spirits

Finally, we have the duality of isolated versus global spirits. This is a distinction I first saw made by Jason Miller, and he uses it to refer to spirits that can be isolated to a single location, rather than those that can exist in multiple locations at the same time. An example of an isolated spirit would be a shade of the dead, which is typically found either in the home of the spirit when they occupied a body or in a graveyard. These spirits are often the cause of hauntings when they do not wish to leave their earthly homes. However, due to their nature as isolated spirits, they can be banished or exorcized, resulting in the ending of the haunting. Global spirits, on the other hand, cannot be isolated to a single location, simply due to their fame and power. Gods, demons, angels, and other well-known spirits fall into this category. This can be observed when two magicians simultaneously conjure the same demon and the demon manifests in both ritual spaces. All of these dualities work hand in hand and can be stacked, so to speak. Therefore, it can be said that greater spirits are global, and can fall into the categories of dark, light, hot, or cold, and so on.

Aside from these dualities, there are other ways to classify spirits. For instance, many of these spirits that you will see in books concerning spirit work will be existing beings. However, spirits can also be created, which we will discuss in depth in a later chapter. But even created spirits can be classified using these dualities. For instance, a spirit created with the energy of Saturn will classify as a lesser, isolated, dark, hot spirit. This is due to the fact that Saturn is considered a planet of dark influence, and its power takes action quickly. But, because you are the only magician feeding energy into this created spirit, it will not be strong enough to manifest in two places at once. This makes it a lesser spirit, and an isolated spirit.

Going back to a point made earlier, your research will help you determine the nature of the spirit you are working with. These will also be the things you look for in your research. The spirit you wish to contact will be determined by either your desire to work with a particular spirit, or by the need that needs to be filled. But once you have established which spirit you are contacting, and have classified it properly, you will know how best to work with it. You would not, for instance, want to try to call an isolated spirit without a singular place for it to manifest for you. But, now that you have an idea of the classifications of spirits, let us move forward into some practical application methods for working with these spirits.

Practical Work

Perform the consecrations of your tools, if you do not already have tools prepared. Then do some research on a spirit you would like to work with. Make plenty of notes and start making lists of correspondences about the spirit, so that when it is time to conjure, you are sufficiently prepared.

CHAPTER II

The Nature of Offerings

B efore we truly dive into the meat of this work, it is important to cover something that is of utmost importance to spirit work: offerings. After all, why would they want to do anything for us if we aren't willing to sacrifice a bit for them? In order to truly understand the need for offerings, we must first look at the four primary classifications of spirit that we deal with during offering ceremonies. I know, I know, we already dealt with classifications earlier, but these are a different set of parameters, specifically made for offerings. The reason for this is that, unlike our previous classification system, these parameters are dynamic, they depend solely upon us and our relationships with the spirits we deal with, rather than being universal. The classifications of spirits we deal with, then, are:

1. *Spirits to which we owe a debt*: Into this category fall spirits we have angered somehow, or that have done us favors without taking gifts first. We often find these spirits troubling our lives because we may have run over their favorite plant or animal, or built a home in a place they find sacred. When this occurs,

the spirit becomes unsettled and will often attach itself to whoever has committed the wrong.

2. *Spirits that we wish to gain the favor of:* These are generally spirits that we have not angered, but have not worked with either. In this category, we find spirits we wish to build a foundation with, and so are doing our research on to build a relationship.

3. *Spirits with which we are neutral:* These spirits are the general spirit populace, those we neither owe a debt to nor have great favor with. Generally, these are spirits we have not worked with or encountered, or have worked with for some time and the relationship is fairly even.

4. *Spirits with which we have favor:* This group of spirits generally contains our ancestors, guardians, personal deities, and other spirits directly tied to ourselves and our paths. These are the spirits we've worked with enough to gain great favor with, those we've spent time developing relationships with, and those that act as our guardian spirits and protectors.

Generally speaking, all spirits will fall into one of these four categories. To determine which category best fits the spirit you're dealing with, you only have to ask what your relationship is like. Is this a spirit you've known for some time, or have you only just started working together? Is this spirit troubling you, or are you at peace? Will this spirit help you if you ask, or does it not even know your name? If you are unsure, treat the spirit as though they are in the first category and work to make peace with them.

When making your offerings to more than one spirit, or to more than a small select team, they can go to any of these groups, or all four at once, though if you're offering to all four, you should always honor the fourth group first, and then work your way down. That way, your guardians are appeased first and foremost, and they will be more than happy to help deal with any rambunctious spirits that try to cause trouble during the ceremony.

With that out of the way, let us look now at the four types of offerings that can be performed. As usual, these are broad strokes at best, but they will give a good idea of what different offerings mean.

Minor Offerings

A minor offering is something small, simple, something that only takes a few minutes to do at most. Generally speaking, a minor offering may consist, at most, of one physical offering such as a candle or stick of incense, an offering of energy, and perhaps a small prayer or invocation to direct the energy toward its intended source. Minor offerings are generally only directed at a single spirit, or a focused group, such as your ancestors, your guides, or one of the above classifications.

Standard Offerings

A standard offering generally has one or two physical offerings, as well as a small ceremony to address the intended recipient or recipients of the offering. This type of offering may be directed toward a single spirit, or an entire classification of spirits.

Major Offerings

Major offerings tend to have a few physical offerings and are generally directed toward two or more classifications of spirits. These offerings are accompanied by a ritualized ceremony. An example may be an offering to all spirits to which you owe a debt, as well as to your guardians, to ensure protection from all negativity, during which you may lay out candles, incense, drink, food, and flowers.

Grand Offerings

Grand offerings are not needed nearly as often as others, but sometimes, the timing just feels right. A grand offering will address all four classifications of spirit, or in other words, all spirits you have dealt with in the past and currently work with, and all spirits you are interested in gaining favor from. This offering will be a substantial ceremony, and will draw upon as many physical offerings as possible. For a grand offering, you may choose to honor one spirit or type of spirit as the main recipient of the offering and decorate your temple in their honor, as well as placing a table out that is laden with offerings of all kinds to appeal to all tastes.

So what things constitute physical offerings? Well, going back to the last chapter, research is key. Study the spirits you have in mind and gather offerings based upon your research. But generally speaking, some of the things you will come across are candles, incense, perfumes, alcohol, water, fruit, vegetables, meat, coins, sex, talismans, jewelry, and art. When it comes to things like sex, they typically desire the energy raised from the act of intercourse, so you could dedicate your next conquest to their name, but in some cases, sexual fluid is acceptable and even preferable.

Now, when it comes to the matter of perishables such as food and flowers, you don't want these things to rot in your temple (or you might—again, do your research). In those instances, a good practice is to let them sit on your altar for a full day, then remove them and dispose of them in nature, or in the domain of the spirit you are honoring. Things such as talismans should be kept with the spirit, or with their effigy, unless directed otherwise. When it comes to money, the money is no longer yours once it is offered, so the best thing to do is to either leave it out in the wild for the spirits to guide where it should go, or else to donate to a charity pleasing to the spirit.

Another important point to raise in the matter of food and drink is it isn't yours. Do not consume it once it is offered. In some traditions, this is acceptable, but in most cases, it is not. It is more acceptable, if the spirit wishes to share, to have your own portion set aside that is not part of what is offered. For instance, when offering to Exu da Capa Preta, I will pour two shots of alcohol. One is for him, and I do not touch it. The other is mine, and I consume it alongside him.

Another word worth mentioning when it comes to symbols and such is that size doesn't matter. In other words, if you are offering to Ares, and you wish to give him a sword, you don't have to give him a full hand and a half sword. He will be just as happy with a dagger or even a toy sword, because it is the imagery, energy, and intent that matters, rather than the actual size of the object. And finally, do not allow a spirit to demand what you are not willing to give. If they are demanding an offering that is simply not possible for you to give, explain this to them, and ask them what else would be acceptable. If they are adamant, then you have a choice to make: Find a way to make the offering, or else find another spirit to deal with. Remember, you are a magician. You run your life; you don't let the disincarnated masses dictate your actions.

All that said, we can move forward to timing. When should we do which offerings? How frequently? What time of day is best? (The last one is a trick question—it depends entirely on your schedule, as well as your research on the spirits you're working with.) There is no specific schedule for when to do which offerings, truthfully, but a good rule of thumb is that you can make a minor offering daily, a standard offering weekly, a major offering monthly, and a grand offering quarterly. These aren't set in stone, but speaking strictly from a financial standpoint, any more than that and you might need a second mortgage to keep your spirits fed. Now, during an immersion cycle, you may want to have more frequent standard and major offerings, but other than that, I'd recommend sticking with that schedule until you can find something that works for you and your spirits.

Now, location is sometimes taken for granted, but I feel it appropriate to mention here. Where does one perform their offerings? More often than not, offerings are done in the temple as a matter of convenience, and the temple is made to appeal to the spirit in question, or at least contains a consecrated effigy. However, there are certain occasions where this may not be the case. For instance, some djinn may only be conjured in specific places, and the spirits of the dead may appreciate not having to travel outside of their resting places too far. In these instances, you can make your offerings in the spirit's home domain. However, special consideration must be taken during these occasions. You don't want to leave behind trash, nor do you want a stray candle to cause a forest fire. Plan for these occasions well in advance to make sure you can pack your materials in easily, make your offerings undisturbed, and pack back out, leaving nothing behind except energy, footsteps, and perhaps some perishable offerings. In the case of candles, you will have to remain behind until the candle burns out. Food, flowers, and such may be left where they are. Things like jewelry, if offered, should either be left with the spirit (placed on the gravestone, wrapped around a tree branch, etc.) or buried. Drink should be poured out on the ground. You get the idea, leave the area in the same condition as when you arrived. The last thing you want is your entire ceremony undermined because the spirit of the forest you were making an offering to got angry over a paper plate left out in the wild.

With all other considerations handled, we turn now to the biggest question left: How do we actually go about performing an offering? Well, that depends on a lot of factors, but it comes down to checking all of the boxes we just laid out. What classification (or classifications) of spirit are you offering to? What type of offering is it? What are you giving, and where? Why are you doing it? Each of these has an impact on the specifications of the offering, but the general ceremony will stay roughly the same. For the sake of example, everything below will be written as though you are doing this in your temple, but feel free to make adjustments as necessary.

For a minor offering, one would begin by having an effigy of the spirit in question on their altar. If, instead of focusing on a single spirit, you are focusing on a specific classification, then ignore the effigy. Set out a candle and a stick of incense and light them. Allow the incense to build a little so that you have a small cloud, and then focus on the target of your offering. Address them with something along the lines of:

Spirits, I make this offering of light and fumigation to you,
that you may receive it well.
Let us be allies now and forever.

And that's it. Your offering is, by all accounts, complete. I personally tend to reserve this sort of offering for spirits I'm close to already, as opposed to those to which I owe a debt or that I am trying to gain favor from, simply because this is not a big deal, and if I'm trying to win them over, I want it to be a big deal.

For standard offerings and above, it is best to put a little more into it, and that is best done by beginning with a cleansing and consecration of the offering. This is a simple step, but an important one. My favorite is an elemental incantation, but work with what suits your style best. My practice is to hold my hands above the offerings and visualize the elements flowing through them in turn, accompanied by the incantation:

By the purest fire, which burns away all that is impure,
By the purest water, which cleanses these vessels,
By purest earth, which creates and holds these forms,
By purest air, which breathes the breath of life,
I declare these offerings sacred and prepared.

I then visualize pure energy flowing into them, which allows them to take the form most pleasing to the spirits, and I say:

May the essence of these gifts
Be more than the sum of their parts,
And may they be pleasing to those who receive them.
May they become that which my guests desire most,
And may they fulfill all needs.

After this, the offerings are prepared for the work.

Standard offerings are only a small step up. Once you have consecrated your offerings, place them on your altar, light any candles or incense, and focus on your guests. For standard offerings, I use a slightly more complex conjuration, like this one, which is aimed specifically at spirits to which I owe debt:

Arise! Arise, all you spirits to whom I owe debt!
Arise, all you spirits whom I have angered!
Arise, all you spirits that hold a grudge against me!
Arise, all you spirits whom I have offended!
Arise, hear my voice, and come!
I conjure you to this place,
at this time, to settle our debts peacefully!
Take these offerings and may they
become that which pleases you the most!

Take your fill, and let us be at peace!

After this, I allow some time for the spirits to take in the gifts laid out for them. When I feel the time has come, I will then give a simple dismissal:

Our time together is at an end!
Be filled, be at peace, and return to
the place from which you came!
Our time here is over, and let it be so peacefully.

This dismissal tells your guests that the offering is done, and warns that if they do not go peacefully, then they will be forcefully removed, though we will cover this in a later chapter.

Major offerings are not so different, except that you may have a lengthier conjuration. You will most certainly have more offerings laid out, and if you wish to direct your conjuration toward a specific spirit, you will want to write something that is suited to them. For instance, if you were offering to spirits to which you owe a debt, but also to the Morrigan, you might add an incantation like this one to your call:

Arise, phantom queen!
Arise, triple goddess of mystery and magick!
Arise, Morrigan, war goddess, giver and taker of life!
Arise, and be welcomed into my space!
See the gifts laid before you.
May they become what you most desire, and may they fill you!
Arise, come and partake of my offerings!
I call you into this place to receive gifts!
Come and be filled!

And as before, you will want to give a proper dismissal upon completion of the offerings.

Grand offerings, as the name implies, step things up greatly. For these, you will want to lay out a full spread. Candles, incense, food, drinks, and anything else you wish to offer. One thing I suggest is to have separate sections to deal with each of the classifications of spirits. This makes it easy to make offerings to them separately, and to keep away potentially wrathful spirits from the main offering area. Once you have your spread and have cleansed your offerings, you are ready to perform the conjuration. Light your candles and incense, and then recite:

> *Spirits of land and sea! Spirits of fire and air!*
> *Those in between, those beyond the veil and those within it!*
> *Arise! Arise and hear my voice!*
> *Spirits who bear me a grudge, spirits to whom I bear a grudge!*
> *Arise! Arise and hear my voice!*
> *Ancestors, guides, guardians, gods!*
> *Patrons and protectors of my path! Arise!*
> *Arise, and hear my voice!*
> *Let every spirit who can hear arise and answer my call!*
> *Come! Come, clean and unclean spirits!*
> *Come, elementals, ghosts, wraiths, and revenants!*
> *Come, angels, demons, and those between!*
> *Come, spirits, and partake!*
> *Take these offerings, and may they take the form*
> *that is most pleasing to you!*
> *Come, take your fill, and let us be at peace!*

Fair warning, a conjuration like this will get a lot of attention, so if you are not spiritually prepared to deal with this much activity, I would suggest holding off on this particular incantation until you are. You may, of course, alter the words to suit your purposes, but being as this is a grand offering, your goal is more than likely to offer to a wide array of spirits, and this incantation does exactly that. And, as before, when the time has come, give a proper dismissal. With a grand offering, it is more likely that you may have some unintended guests left afterward, and in this case, you will need to banish them.

Once your offerings are complete, you can either end your session if your only goal is making offerings, or, if your goal is spell work, move into the next phase of your ritual. Your spirits being properly fed, they will be more than happy to set to work on whatever it is you wish to call them for. However, there is another use for offerings that is worth mentioning. After your offerings are made, but before the dismissal, you are sharing space with your spiritual community. This is the perfect time to meditate and connect with the beings around you. I particularly like doing this when I am offering to my guardians and guides, but it can be done with any spirit or group of spirits. Jake Stratton-Kent refers to this practice as a "night in with the boys," and is a worthy endeavor all on its own. There are even certain traditions where this is all that is done at certain levels. You feed your spirits, sit in congress with them, share your thoughts and listen for theirs, and then move on. You can also use this time for divination with the spirits, whether to learn something of the future or simply to commune. Truthfully, the time during an offering is one of the most intimate times you will have with your spirits, and it is worth taking advantage of this fact.

Practical Work

Perform some offerings with your spirits. Start with minor and standard offerings to the fourth category of spirits and sit with them in congress. Make note of your experiences for future reference.

CHAPTER III

Spirit Senses

I feel that it is only natural, in a text devoted to working with spirits, to discuss the nature of spirit senses. This section entirely skipped my mind during the creation of the first edition, and I have kicked myself for that ever since. Therefore, this entire chapter is devoted to correcting that mistake, and there is nowhere better to start such a discussion than with a definition of what spirit senses are, what they are not, and what senses are most typically called upon in spirit communication sessions.

Most of the time, when I am discussing the nature of spirit senses to someone who claims to be unable, for whatever reason, to commune with the spirit world, we eventually reach the same conclusion every time: Their perception of spirit communication is vastly different from reality. It is apparently common belief that those who possess the ability to communicate with spirits do so as though the spirits are physical people coming by for a visit. The popular idea is that clairvoyance allows them to see the spirit as though they are sitting across the table, sharing a cup of tea, or that clairaudience means they can hear them as though on a phone call. However, I have rarely found that to be the case.

I have found that spirit communication tends to be more of a gentle whisper as opposed to a shout. The little voice in the back of your head, the tingling down your neck, the shadow at the corner of your eye, these are all ways the spirit communicates with us. The trick is learning to recognize what is spirit and what is us. Meditation can be useful here. Meditation teaches us to recognize our own thoughts and distractions and release them, and by learning to recognize our own thoughts, we also learn to distinguish those that come from the spirit world. But before we launch into that, we must first turn our eyes to the spirit senses themselves.

The five primary spiritual senses correspond directly to the five physical senses. The physical sense of sight corresponds to clairvoyance, or psychic sight. This word means "clear sight," and is an apt description. The physical sense of hearing corresponds to clairaudience, or psychic hearing. This word means "clear hearing," and is a highly sought-after skill. The physical sensation of touch corresponds to clairsentience, or psychic feeling. This word means "clear feeling," but it also extends to phenomena like empathy, or sensing the emotions of others. The physical sense of taste corresponds to clairgustance, or psychic tasting. And the physical sense of smell corresponds to clairalience, or psychic smelling. These last two are not as sought after, though they can be quite useful in certain situations. However, as the methods for developing them do not differ so much from the others, we will not spend time on them. If you wish to develop your clairgustance or clairalience, the information provided here can be modified to do so. For now, we will focus solely on the big three: clairvoyance, clairaudience, and clairsentience.

Now, as we have already stated, meditation is the key to these abilities, so we will start there. There are many ways to meditate, and none is better or more important than the others, but one of the best forms of meditation to practice initially is zazen, or no mind meditation. This technique focuses on nothing but your breath, releasing all distractions as soon as they arise. The difficulty arises in developing the focus required for this technique. It is easy to learn, but impossible to truly master. However, as long as we keep trying, then we have not failed. In fact, people tend to think that if they get distracted, they have stopped meditating, when in reality they have grasped the meaning of meditation. When we meditate and a distraction arises that we notice, we are faced with a choice. If we can ignore and release the distraction and return to meditation, then we have truly succeeded. If, however, we pursue the distraction, then meditation has ended and we have returned to our normal lives.

But how is no mind meditation practiced? The first considera-tion in meditation in general is position. We've all seen images of monks sitting in full or half lotus, legs crossed in seemingly impossi-ble manners, and this is indeed an ideal position. However, in order to properly sit in even half lotus, a certain degree of flexibility is required. An acceptable alternative to this is to sit "criss-cross apple-sauce," as they say. In any of these poses, I highly recommend using a pillow or cushion to provide a measure of comfort during your session. This also will help with keeping correct posture, which is important for both physical and spiritual reasons. You can also use a personal favorite position of mine, which is called the dragon pose. This position is a kneeling posture, knees together, with your feet straight so that the tops of your feet are resting on the floor. Placing your hands on your knees will help maintain balance. You may also choose to meditate from a seated position, so long as your feet are flat on the floor and your back is straight. You could also choose to meditate lying down, though this is not recommended as, due to the relaxing nature of meditation, you may find yourself dozing off.

After you have settled on your posture, the next consideration is your focus. There are multiple focuses you could use, though some favorites are images of deities, colors, symbols, and peaceful imagery if you wish for a visual focus; white noise, forest or ocean sounds, relaxing music, singing bowls, and bells if you prefer an auditory focus; mantras, prayers, and chants if you want a vocal focus; or mudras, gestures, and yoga poses if you wish for a more tactile focus. However, in the beginning, the best focus is one you already possess: your breath. Count your breaths, in and out, until you reach ten, and then begin again. This simple, repetitive counting will help you relax and give you a focus that is easy to use so that you do not have to fear distraction from some of the more in-depth focuses available.

The next consideration is timing, both of the length of the session and the actual time of the schedule. Some people can wake up early enough to get their daily meditation in before they start their day, while others prefer to use meditation as a way to unwind before bed. Still others like to use it as a way to take a break from their day to refresh their mind before going back to work, or whatever they have going on. Personally, I like to use all three: a quick morning meditation to reconsider my dreams and look for messages, an afternoon meditation to refresh myself, and a longer evening session to quiet my mind and order my thoughts before retiring. Whatever schedule you choose, it is best to keep it consistent to develop discipline and to form the habit. The length of the session is also important. In the beginning, most find it difficult to meditate for more than a few minutes at a time before giving in to distraction, and that is fine. We all start somewhere. The important thing is that you start. I recommend starting with three to five minutes per day and gradually working your way into longer sessions. Set a timer and focus only on your breath until the timer dings. A timer relieves you of the need to check the time every thirty seconds to see how good you are doing.

Once you have gotten your pose, focus, and schedule figured out, it's time for the fun part: meditating! Set your timer, assume your chosen pose and breathe deeply. As you allow yourself to breathe deeper, relax your muscles. The most effective method for this comes from hypnosis, and that is to focus on a particular muscle or muscle group and tense it as hard as you can, hold it for a moment, and then very intentionally relax those muscles. Do this for your entire body as you continue your deep breathing and you will quickly find yourself in a deeply relaxed state. Once you've done this, allow your eyes to gently close (unless you are using a visual focus, in which case simply relax them and gaze softly at your focus), and then begin counting your breaths. Count one for the in breath, two for the out breath, and so on until you reach ten, then begin again. Continue this until your timer goes off. If you find yourself following an errant thought or getting disturbed by some outside noise, simply acknowledge this distraction, release it, and return to your counting. That's all it takes to begin a meditation practice!

You can also look into things such as tai chi or qigong if you want to take up moving meditation, or look up various mudras to meditate with, but I won't belabor those points here as that is not the purpose of this volume. Instead, we will move forward with exercises to expand your spirit senses. But first, let us look at the core concept that runs through all three: intuition. Clairvoyance is, in its most basic form, empowered visualization meeting with intuition. Clairaudience is that voice in the back of your head running on intuition. Clairsentience is using intuition to know when the goosebumps are from the spirits or the cold. So without a developed sense of intuition, nothing else will be useful to you.

Developing a sense of intuition is a tricky art, but worth it. One of the best ways to begin this process is by asking questions. These questions can be directed at the spirit world, at your higher self, or the universe in general, and you don't even need to specify to whom they are directed. You only need to ask and trust the answer you get. After a meditation session, focus on something that you will be able to check on afterward. Ask yourself about something specifically that may or may not occur, and trust your first impulse. Then verify your results, because without verification, you're simply guessing. For instance, if you meditate before work, ask yourself (or the universe, or your spirit guides, or whoever) about a detail at work. For instance, you might ask, "Will Sandra call out today?" You will have an immediate gut feeling, as we all do when contemplating things like this. The difference is, you are asking this from a point of pure openness, having just meditated, so your intuition will be in tune. Once you get to work, you can then find out whether or not you were right.

Another, albeit more subjective method, is to get a piece of paper and pen, and immediately after a meditation session, ask yourself something out loud, such as "What do I need in my life right now?" Repeat the question three times, then write the first thing that comes into your head. Pursue whatever it is you were drawn to write and find out if it actually is what you needed. You can use this method as a form of divination as well, asking the universe about future events and then seeing how they play out.

For developing the skills necessary to combine with intuition to form your spirit senses, we will refer to an old favorite technique that I have used with students for years: the orange method. The first thing you will need is an orange. Go get yourself some fruit, and if you can't get an orange, any other fruit will suffice. But for the sake of this example, we will stay with the orange. First up is sight: Observe your orange. Pick it up and turn it about, really taking in its appearance from all sides. Does it have a stem? Are there any blemishes? Does the light reflect off of it in any special way? Take note of everything. Then, after you've committed the orange to memory, close your eyes and recreate the orange in your mind's eye. Make sure you get all the details. When you have finished imagining your orange, open your eyes and see how close your mental image was. Work with this exercise until you can perfectly visualize it every time.

Next up is the sense of touch: clairsentience. Hold your orange in your hands and run your fingers over it. Feel the curves, bumps, and wrinkles in its skin. Feel for any spots that are tough or soft. Commit its feeling to memory. Then, put the orange down, close your eyes, and recreate in your mind the sensation of feeling the orange. It helps if you combine this with your visualization techniques so that you can see, in a way, what you are touching. Again, compare your imagined sensations to the physical orange, and continue this exercise until you can perfectly recall the feeling of the orange.

Finally, we have clairaudience. You may be wondering how that works with an orange, and you would not be entirely off base. Our options are limited, but they exist nonetheless. When it comes to practicing clairaudience, you will do things like scratch the orange, peel it, bounce it off a wall, anything to make it make noise. Then, as before, you will mentally recreate the sensation until you can do it perfectly. An alternative to this is to use music instead of an orange, and most of us can do that anyway. How many times have you heard the opening notes of a favorite song, and immediately recalled the music in your own mind?

Once you have achieved proficiency in any of these skills, you can begin to apply your intuition. For instance, during an offering, you may feel the presence of a spirit and want to know how it appears. So, closing your eyes, you will ask it to show itself to you, and you will instantly see an image in your head. You could write this off to imagination or wishful thinking, but if you have been sharpening your skills with these exercises, you can be confident that you are receiving what the spirit is transmitting. All it takes is practice. Now, one question I have been asked a lot is, "But I can't visualize, so how can I communicate with spirits?" Well, that is why we discussed multiple types of spirit sense. It is entirely possible that when you close your eyes, no matter how hard you try, all you see is darkness. That is fine! You still have your clairsentience and clairaudience to draw upon. Not being adept at one or even two senses is not a crippling issue, and if anything, this gives you a goal to work toward. So, in summation, meditation allows you to clear your mind and recognize your own thoughts. Intuition allows you to receive messages that you can differentiate from your own thoughts because of intuition. And the spirit senses provide filters through which that information can come in whichever method suits your style the most.

Practical Work

Begin developing a meditation practice and working on your intuition and spirit senses. Make it a point to meditate for at least three minutes, practice your intuition, and work at developing at least one form of spirit sense every day.

CHAPTER IV

Magickal Invocation

The art of invocation is the act of calling a spirit into yourself for the purpose of deeper communion, while staying outside of the realm of possession. Possession could be said to be the deepest form of invocation, but that is a distinction that shall be discussed later. Invocation is typically reserved for greater spirits, as well as global spirits. It can be used to work with other classifications of spirits, but it is preferred for these particular classes because the level of power that these spirits exude is typically too great to be contained during an evocation; therefore, invocation is the better method. An invocation is like a prayer. In fact, the definition of invocation is prayer, merely directed at a specific force for a specific purpose.

The invocation litany typically contains references to the many aspects of the spirit being called, and then calls the spirit into the body of the magician. This is always done as a request rather than a demand, because the spirit being invoked is typically not going to take well to being commanded. An example of an invocation of the Morrigan would look like this:

Morrigan, mother of the night, the three in one,

and yet singular goddess.
You rule and reign over the night,
and the dead call you Mother.
You are the raven that flies above the battlefield,
guiding the souls of fallen warriors into the cauldron.
You are the mistress of magick,
the queen of illusion, the dark mother.
Your prowess in battle is unmatched,
and those who serve you fear neither blade nor arrow.
Hear my call this night and enter my temple.
Fill this place with your presence
and allow me to feel your heart.
Join with me, and allow my hands to be your hands,
allow my tongue to be your tongue,
and allow my heart to beat with your heart.

Similarly, an invocation of Saint Michael might go something like this:

Saint Michael, protect me in my hour of need,
and defend me against all forces that would rise against me.
Let me feel your presence around me
as I bask in the warmth that you bring.
Be with me now, and shield me with your sword as you
strike away all who would strike me down.
Be with me now, and allow me to use your power to
protect myself and my home from the forces of the enemy.

These are only examples of invocations, however, so feel free to use them or to create your own. Invocation is typically used to call upon the power of a spirit to imbue an object with energy, and create a talisman. It is also used to transmit information from either the spirit to the magician or from the spirit to another person through the magician. However, there are a multitude of uses for this skill. One such use is to invoke a spirit of authority and success before a job interview. Going into the interview while bearing the presence of the spirit will increase your chances of impressing the potential employer and landing the job.

So how exactly does invocation work? Quite simply, it is an appeal to a higher power to use your body as a vessel of sorts to work for your will. Another term used for invocation is *godform assumption*, if that helps to clarify the purpose behind the practice. As far as the specifics of invocation, that will differ depending on the tradition and the spirit being summoned, but there are some things that are universal. First, no invocation is done without giving an offering. Second, when performing an invocation, the entity that is being invoked will typically be the central, or only, being in your ritual, so your altar should be adorned only with imagery and correspondence of that entity. Thirdly, the incantation should not only call upon the entity, but extoll the virtues that you wish to invoke. Often, deities are the subjects of invocations, and they have multiple aspects. You may only require one aspect of the deity, so that is the one you will focus on.

Honestly, though, it is the invocation prayer itself that is most important in invocation. It does not have to be overly ritualized, and in fact, the simpler the better in most cases. An invocation can be as simple as lighting a candle and reciting a prayer to your deity before going about your day. This may only give a light charge, but that may be all you really need to get through the day. In any case, since the incantation itself is the most important aspect of invocation, it is best if it is written by you to suit your needs. As long as the incantation expresses your desire to connect to that entity's aspect, and appropriate offerings are given, your invocation will be successful.

Once you have some familiarity with invocation, it can also be worked into your immersion cycle when appropriate. Additionally, it can be worked into your offerings. When using invocation in tandem with offerings, the spirit will often guide you in the work. Sometimes, this may mean that the spirit is invoked and then consumes the offerings using your body, and sometimes it may simply mean that the spirit enjoys the presence of the offerings once you have given them and then performed the invocation. This will depend largely upon your personal practice, as well as the spirit in question.

A Sample Invocation to the Morrigan

Your immersion phase will include the chanting of her name, as well as the names of the three goddesses who form her trinity: Macha, Anu, and Babd. Additionally, you will meditate on the symbol of the triskele, as well as the symbol of the three ravens, both of which are closely associated with the Morrigan. You will light a dragon's blood novena candle and allow it to burn completely out, starting a new one every time one candle completes. You will also burn dragon's blood incense every day alongside the candle. Additionally, you will perform an offering to the Morrigan every few days, which will include the dragon's blood incense and candle, as well as whatever offering you choose to give. Some of her favorite offerings include dark beer, apples, the feathers of the crow or raven, and daggers or swords dedicated to her. After at least thirty days of this immersion cycle, you will arrange your temple with red and black cloth, images of crows and ravens, a triskele symbol, and the blades that were dedicated to her. You will perform another offering ceremony, and when it is completed, you will perform the invocation that you have written or else use one that you have found. If you do not find an invocation that you like, you are free to use the example invocation given previously. As you recite the invocation litany, you will mark upon yourself the symbol of the triskele, and you may wish to draw three ravens upon yourself. This marking of yourself with the symbols corresponding to the Morrigan will be useful in drawing her closer to you. You may have to recite the invocation several times before solid contact is made, but this is normal. Do not worry. Instead, focus on drawing her closer to you through your signs of dedication and through your invocation. When contact has been made, and you feel the presence of the Morrigan around you, you may use this time to commune with her, ask questions, and perform ritual work with her power and authority.

Invocation is a very intimate form of spirit work. The only form that goes deeper than invocation is the art of possession, and possession can be said to be invocation taken to its deepest level. The primary difference between invocation and possession, at least on the surface, is that during invocation, you retain consciousness, while during possession, the spirit takes control of your body. This is not a perfect distinction, but it is close enough to give you an idea of how they are different.

Another difference between possession and invocation is that invocation is typically used to channel the power of a deity for the purpose of communion with another, or the charging of an item. Possession, on the other hand, is used when direct action from the spirit is requested. These two distinctions may occasionally be reversed, but generally speaking, these are useful distinctions. An example of this is the comparison of the Bornless One ritual to a Vodoun ritual. The Bornless One ritual invokes within the magician the authority of the Divine itself to accomplish a task. This is often used for the purposes of protection, authority, and empowering an object. There are other uses for this ritual, but generally speaking they are all simply applications of energy through authority. However, Vodoun rituals typically make use of position so that the spirit may reach into the lives of those attending the ritual and effect change.

Of course, now that I have mentioned it, I must share with you the Bornless One ritual. This ritual has roots in the Golden Dawn, though it was created based upon an older Greek ritual. I have personally used this ritual many times, and it has always proven to be quite powerful. There are a myriad of ways that this ritual can be used, so I inspire you to use your creativity when working with it. However, one of its primary forms is protection. This ritual brings you into alignment with the current of the divine itself, and when in alignment with this current, your word becomes law in the physical world.

Knowing that, you may use this ritual, and then use the divine current that is now flowing within you to create a shield that will be very difficult for your enemies to penetrate. This is but one idea, however, so feel free to explore and test this method for yourself. With that said, here is the Bornless One ritual:

AOTH ABRAOTH BAYM ISAK SABAOTH IAO
I summon thee, the Bornless One:
Thee that didst create the earth and the heavens,
Thee that didst create the night and the day,
Thee that didst create the darkness and the light,
Thou art OSORONNOPHRIS
whom no man hath seen at any time.
Thou art IABAS. Thou art IAPOS.
You have distinguished between the just and the unjust.
You have made the female and the male.
You have revealed the seed and the fruit.
You have made men to love one another and to hate one another.

I am thy prophet unto whom thou didst transmit thy arcana,
the whole quintessence of magic.
Thou didst produce the moist and the dry,
and that which nourishes all created life.
I am the messenger of OSORONNOPHRIS!
This is thy true name handed down to the prophets:
ARBATHIAO REIBET ATHELEBERSET ARA BLATHA
ALBEU EBENPHI CHI CHITASGIE IBAOTH IAO
Hear me and make all spirits subject unto me so that every
spirit of the firmament and of the ether, upon the earth and
under the earth, on dry land and in the water, of whirling
air and rushing fire, and every spell and scourge of
God may be obedient unto me.
I call upon thee with an empty spirit,
oh awesome and invisible god.
AROGOGOROBRAO SOCHOU
MODORIO PHALRCHAO OOO
Hear me and make all spirits subject unto me so that every
spirit of the firmament and of the ether,
upon the earth and under the earth,
on dry land and in the water, of whirling air and rushing fire,
and every spell and scourge of God may be obedient unto me.
Holy Bornless One hear me!
ROUBRIAO MARI ODAM BAABNA BAOTH
ASS ADONAI APHNIAO ITHOLETH ABRASAX AEOOY
Hear me and make all spirits subject unto me so that every
spirit of the firmament and of the ether,
upon the earth and under the earth,
on dry land and in the water, of whirling air and rushing fire,
and every spell and scourge of God may be obedient unto me.
MABARRAIO IOEL KOTHA ATHERE BALO ABRAOTH
Hear me and make all spirits subject unto me so that every

spirit of the firmament and of the ether, upon the earth
and under the earth, on dry land and in the water,
of whirling air and rushing fire,
and every spell and scourge of God may be obedient unto me
AOTH ABRAOTH BASYM ISAK SABAOTH IAO!
He is the lord of the gods! He is the lord of the world!
He is the one whom the winds fear!
He is the one who made all things by the command of his voice!
Lord, King, Master, Helper, empower my soul
IEOU PYR IOU PYR IAOT IAEO IOOU ABRASAX
SABRIAM OO YY AY OO YY ADONAI
IDE EDE Good messenger of God!
ANLALA LAI GAIA DIACHARNA CHORYN

(Here, allow the energy you've raised to enter you and take you over as the Bornless One is invoked into your body. Note the change in perspective of the final part of the litany.)

I am the Bornless One with sight in the feet,
strong in the immortal fire!
I am the truth that hates that evil is wrought in the world!
I am the one that makes the lightning
flash and the thunder roll!
I am the one whose sweat is heavy rain which falls
upon the earth, making it fertile.
I am the one whose mouth is utterly aflame!
I am the destroyer and begetter!
I am the grace of the Aeon!
The Heart Girt with a Serpent is my name!
Come forth and follow me so that every spirit of the
firmament and of the ether,
upon the earth and under the earth,

on dry land and in the water,
of whirling air and rushing fire,
and every spell and scourge of God may be obedient unto me.
IAO SABAOTH!

At first, this ritual may seem daunting, but as you perform it more and more, it will become more comfortable to you. Additionally, the energy of the Bornless One will become familiar and relaxing to you as you perform this invocation with regularity. You will notice that the final aspect of this ritual is not spoken as a magician call into the deity, but as the deity who has taken residence within the body of the magician. This is one of the finest examples of invocation and one of the most potent. This ritual was modified by Aleister Crowley, and though he attempted to give meaning to the barbarous words in this ritual, it has been typically understood that they are simply the names of the Divine, or at least a bit of a mantra designed to draw you closer to the Divine. And now that we have taken a good look at invocation, it is time to move forward to one of the most popular applications of spirit work in magick today: evocation.

Practical Work

Begin your research on which spirit you would like to invoke first. Start gathering material and preparing your temple, and when you are ready, perform your invocation.

CHAPTER V

Magickal Evocation

I nvocation tends to be more of a passive art, not requiring as much action on the part of the magician. Evocation, on the other hand, is much more active, usually taking form as a complex ceremony. This is the type of ceremony typically covered in the old grimoires. It is, of course, entirely possible to create your own rituals, but first, it is recommended that you have a working knowledge of the classical methods first. Once you understand the mechanics of the original systems and can confidently dissect them on your own, you are ready to move into the construction of your own rituals. This, by the way, is where the preparation of your implements comes in handy, as they will be quite useful in your rituals.

If you have been practicing magick for any amount of time, you have likely developed your own daily practice that involves meditation, protection, and cleansing. If you are doing these things fairly regularly, you are prepared for evocation on all levels. However, if not, then you need to develop your skills in meditation, and a daily practice of protection and cleansing. Meditation is important in all forms of magick, but especially in spirit work. The point of meditation is to learn to develop your ability to know your own thoughts and to cut out distractions. If you are able to do this, then you can determine what thoughts are yours and what thoughts come from the spirit you are working with.

Keeping up with a practice of saging, spreading Florida water, or any other cleansing practice is an excellent way to keep your space clean of negativity. This also establishes a bit of a clear zone, so that you will be protected from outside influence. This, combined with basic shielding exercises, will allow you to safely interact with outside forces. If you do not have a shielding habit, then a simple shield can be formed by feeling your energy flowing around you, and then solidifying it into a shell. This is a basic visualization exercise, but it is enough for our purposes. With that in mind, let us take a look at the steps of proper evocation: *Preparing the area, the Call, Manifestation, Communion, and Dismissal.*

Anyone who thinks of grimoires will think of the complex circles that are in them. These circles serve two purposes: protecting the magician, and creating an area that focuses the energy of the ritual for the spirit to manifest. In rites evoking demons and other troublesome spirits, protection will certainly be the main purpose. This is why the circles in old grimoires are often filled with names of gods. In other instances, however, the latter is the more prominent concern. Typically, these circles are simply consecrations of the area, creating a wall of protection between you and the spirit. However, there are more in-depth methods that can be used when dealing with particularly dangerous spirits. That being said, it is also worth noting that not all evocation circles have to be that complex. If your authority is solid enough, a simple circle will suffice.

Sometimes, such as with the Goetia triangle, there is a separate place for the spirit to manifest in. Somehow, the image of the circle and triangle has become so well known that many ceremonial magicians think that all evocations work this way, but this is not the case. Usually, the spirit will simply appear at the edge of the circle, or even within it. Even some of the infamous Goetia rituals don't call for the use of the triangle. I personally prefer not to use such acts of separation, save for certain baneful rituals.

As a general rule, unless you are dealing with a truly dangerous being, a simple quarter calling will suffice. However, if you wish for a deeper level of protection, you can take this further. A fine example of this would be to perform the Greater Banishing Ritual of the Pentagram, followed by a cleansing of the area with sage, and then performing the Rite of the Bornless One to declare your space completely safe, and to empower your circle further.

Rituals with angels and other benevolent beings, however, are a bit different. Protection is less of a concern, as these spirits are seen to be helpful, and it is encouraged that they be allowed to stand in your ritual space alongside you. For these friendlier spirits, you want your space to be more conducive to their qualities. For instance, for a spirit of Venus, you'd want to apply as many correspondences of Venus to your ritual as possible. Spirit evocations are invitations to outside entities to enter our plane, and as such, they need to be made to feel welcome, though be mindful that specifics vary from spirit to spirit. This will come down to your research, and is the bulk of the staging section. Whatever spirit you are working with, you have to prepare the area in a way they will be attracted to.

The call, or the conjuration, is the bulk of the ritual itself, the act of calling the spirit forth. There are a variety of rituals of conjuration, with all manner of included implements and protocols. But the two most important elements are the name and seal of the spirit. The reason for this is simple: This is the spirit's calling card. Some will say that to alter any of the original rituals is to open our ritual up to all kinds of disaster, and if we do so out of laziness or ignorance, they are correct. However, if we set them aside or replace them due to our level of understanding, then not only are we safe from disaster, but we have added our personal flair to the ritual and made it our own. Again, this is where familiarity with the original ritual is handy. By knowing what the ritual is made of, you can determine whether or not the original elements are necessary.

Authority is necessary to call spirits from the ether into this world, as the spirits you are calling forth will need to respect you to listen to you. There are many ways to accomplish this. Of course, you can always become an authority figure through energy generation and compression combined with meditation. However, since we are focusing on spirit work, we will look at one of the other options that is particularly effective: invocation. Here is where your research comes into play. In your research, you will find that your spirit will fall under the authority of a higher spirit. This is the spirit that you will invoke to take authority over the spirit that you wish to evoke. For instance, an evocation of Ziku of the *Necronomicon* may make use of an invocation of Marduk, while an evocation of Zazel will instead rely upon Agiel.

No matter how a system is changed, the two things that almost always make it into the ceremony are the name and seal of the spirit. In some ways, the name and seal are the spirit itself, and should be treated with the respect that the spirit deserves. Many magicians have experienced direct spiritual contact by simply drawing the seal, or seeing it in a book, particularly those who are well attuned to the current of the spirit they are attempting to call. This also comes back to the immersion phase, where you have aligned yourself with the spirit through the use of its seal and name as meditative focuses.

Many rituals require the magician to wear the seal as a pendant. This can be as simple as wearing a piece of paper on a chain or creating a clay talisman of the seal. Some magicians prefer to stare intently at the seal, as if they are scrying, but I find that this method is more useful in the immersion phase than in the ritual itself. This method tends to cause spiritual fascination rather than full evocation, and our goal is to have manifestation, not trance-state communion.

The words of the conjuration are always different, primarily by virtue of the magician who recorded them. I have performed many evocations by simply chanting the name of the spirit in question, though typically there is a conjuration made through the authority of a greater being. Some grimoires give huge conjurations, often partially in Latin, Greek, or some other language. It is a common belief that the purpose of this is to fool your conscious mind and get you into an altered state of consciousness. While I believe this theory has some backing, based on my studies in the psychological effects of magick, I believe that these incantations serve a real purpose to bring yourself into alignment with those forces through vibration.

If you have developed your psychic senses and can consciously work with them and activate them, it will not be necessary to enter into a state of altered awareness to communicate with the spirit, but even if you did choose to do so, there are many more effective methods, such as meditation, mantras, energy work, and even exercise, than to resort to mindless chanting. Your conscious mind will likely be more wrapped up trying to get the chants correct than on your ritual in any case.

Another element that is fairly common in evocations is a request to the spirit to manifest in a way that is non-threatening, not frightening, and easy to perceive. These beings are from another dimension, after all, and if they so choose, could manifest in ways that can literally kill you when trying to perceive them. While spirits can manifest in ways that are terrifying and monstrous, it makes it easier on the magician to request that the spirit appear in a manner that is easily perceived and makes sense to our minds. I personally believe that it is imperative to try the classical evocations in their original form, but when writing your own evocations, I encourage you to make the ritual your own, cutting away any unnecessary material.

Generally speaking, there are four stages of manifestation that powerful spirits such as angels and demons can take during ritual. From lowest to highest, these are as follows.

The Shell

This initial level of contact is mostly driven by the magician. This occurs when they have an idea of what the spirit should be, so they form that idea into a shell and fill it with energy, which contains a sliver of the true essence. This is also seen in what I call the first level of divine contact, when you create a shell of a deity based on their qualities and call it forth. This is often mistaken by beginning magicians as the true face of the god, but they are often in for a surprise down the road.

Evocation

This is what we are dealing with presently. Here, you call forth the being, and it chooses its form based on what you requested in the conjuration and how you staged the ritual.

Possession

This is covered in a later chapter, but it is essentially the marriage of evocation and invocation, where the spirit is called forth into the body of a willing host. This is most commonly known as a corner-stone of Vodoun, though it is not the only tradition that makes use of the practice.

Grand Appearance

These are the rare events in which the spirit manifests as fully as your mind can handle. Typically, this is when a magician is not trying to contact the spirit, but the other way around. When the spirits want to get your attention, they do so in such a spectacular way that you cannot deny it.

All that said, we are concerned with number two for the purpose of this chapter. Remember the staging section? This is how we set things up, along with our conjurations, to direct the spirits to manifest in a particular way or place. For example, when dealing with difficult spirits, we can direct them within a triangle such as the one featured in the Goetia. We can also have them appear at the edge of the circle.

In some cases, we may set up a crystal ball, black mirror, or even an incense burner, thick with smoke, for the spirit to use. If the spirit is one we may judge as dangerous, this is best set up outside the circle; otherwise, it can be set up on the altar, as in Trithemius's system, which has been referenced and updated in Frater Rufus Opus's work, *The Modern Angelic Grimoire*. This is an excellent work, by the way, if you are new to evocation and are looking for something traditional to start with.

The thing with evocations is that they don't always go as planned. The spirit may not manifest in the way you wanted. You can try to force it to comply or just go with it. This all comes down to the individual situation. Real magick is not about following written rules, but a living, breathing experience. The spirit may also choose not to manifest at all. If this occurs, you can try to force it with increasingly more threatening evocations, or you can let it go. I have always found that it is best to just let them go. Sometimes, it is a simple matter of perception, distraction, or other intervening circumstances. Should this occur, keep an eye out for this spirit to show signs that it heard, but did not manifest, and try your ritual again on another day.

You should also be aware that whatever form the spirit takes, it is doing so for you, not because it has to. Most of the spirits from grimoires are global spirits, which means that these beings can be everywhere at once. They do not have to manifest in a singular place. They do so simply because we request it.

If something goes wrong and the spirit manifests in ways that are frightening or negatively affecting you, simply ask or command the spirit to take a pleasing shape that is easy to perceive. If the spirit disobeys you, then you can constrain it, or exorcize it, or simply dismiss it. I've never had this happen, but I have heard stories, so be ready, just in case.

I also want to cover the use of seers in the ritual here. Some magicians have used seers because they either didn't have the ability to perceive the spirit, or felt they would have more control if someone was acting as the bridge between them and the spirit. Others do so in order to interact directly with the spirit, and still others do it because they want to see if there is a difference in practice. The tradition of using a seer has a long tradition, and if you wish to work this way, by all means, go for it. I have worked both ways, and I personally prefer to work alone.

After the spirit manifests, ask it whatever you wish and make your requests. You should already know what you are calling the spirit for, and have done your research on its capabilities, long before reaching this stage. There are, however, different methods of communion you may wish to experiment with. Some prefer to use a pendulum, some like spirit boards, and some like to rely on their inner sight. Whichever method you choose, be sure that you are ready to work with it.

Dismissals are fairly simple. Politely thank the being for attending, ask that it heed your calls again in the future, and send it off. When dealing with more aggressive spirits, you may wish to do something more in depth, but that is entirely up to you. Whichever method you choose, remain polite but firm, and make sure that the spirit has left before you end the ritual.

Now that we have seen the steps, let us go through them in practical application. For our purposes, we will use an evocation of Sorath, the planetary spirit of the Sun. To begin, your ritual area will be draped in gold and yellow cloth, and you will have drawn the circle of the Sun from the Greater Key of Solomon on the floor in yellow or gold. Your circle will be surrounded by yellow or gold candles, and if possible, you will have created a hexagonal plate of gold with the seal of Sorath on one side, and the kamea of the Sun on the other. This plate will sit at the center of the circle, with your incense burning on top of it. If this is not possible, a sheet of construction paper will work just as well. When the stage is set, you will invoke the intelligence of the Sun, Nachiel, with an invocation that goes something like this:

> *Nachiel, emissary of the Sun,*
> *flaming spirit of radiance and power,*
> *rise through me, and lend me your strength.*
> *Let the blazing sun shine through my eyes*
> *as my hands move in your power.*

Having made contact and called Nachiel into yourself, you can then make the evocation of Sorath:

> *Sorath, the spirit of force and flame,*
> *I call you into this plane to stand before me*
> *in a form that is comprehensible to my mind,*
> *and speak to me in a clear voice.*
> *Rise into this place, and commune with me,*
> *that my goals may be accomplished.*

Repeat this call, or chant his name, until Sorath manifests for you. When he does, commune with him and go over what it is you wish for him to do for you. When all is finished, dismiss him, saying something like:

> *Thank you, Sorath, for coming to this place.*
> *May we ever be friends. As you came in power, so go in peace.*

Your ritual has ended, and you may now go about your business, trusting Sorath to handle your requests.

As with invocation, the incantations of evocation work best when written yourself. However, that can be a daunting task when you consider that you are no longer writing a request, but by all technicality a command. If you are not yet comfortable with this idea, then by all means, use the traditional evocation of the tradition you are working with. But take notes on the incantations you come across and compare them. See the common threads that make them work, and use these for inspiration in your own writing. Some of the threads you will see are that the calls always take place from a point of authority over the spirit, and they always call upon a higher spirit to command the spirit being evoked. They also name attributes of the entity that they are wanting to use for their work. They promise reward for success and punishment for failure. Keep these things in mind and your incantations will work wonders.

CHAPTER VI

The Nature of Spiritual Pacts

The topic of pact formation is one of the most popular, and of course most misunderstood, topics in the world of black magick. Every day, thousands of magicians around the world facepalm as a newcomer asks the legendary question: How do I sell my soul for fame and power? In fact, many grimoires are reputed to teach how to do this, and yet they never seem to deliver on their promise. But why is that? Well, we'll be examining that shortly, but first we will look at a few other aspects of what pacts really are.

The common misconception, the popular theme of what pacts are believed to be, is simple: Pacts are believed to be a sale, a trade of goods so to speak. And in some sense, they can be, but not in the popularly conceived form: the forfeit of the soul for a goal. No, a pact is an agreement, a bargain with the spirit to gain something in exchange for something else. This is typically dedication or some form of offering, but we will examine the specific types of pacts later in this chapter.

So, getting back to the question: What is a pact? I think it would be good here to address what pacts can be used to achieve. Again, this will be touched on in depth later in this chapter, but a jump start never hurts. First things first, let us look at what they cannot (or at least, have not been recorded to be able to) do:

Immortality: Here's the thing, you can make as many pacts for immortality as you want. But the only way to test them, to really test them, is to not die. And we mostly succeed at that every day. But until time ceases, and you're still here, we won't really know for sure, will we?

Break the Laws of Physics: This category includes things such as growing wings, physically shapeshifting into some other creature, materializing gold from air, and so on. Why? Because short of the most powerful rites in magickal history, the laws of physics may bend ever so slightly, but they do not break. And if you are capable of such feats, then you probably aren't reading this book.

Make you rich overnight: Make no mistake, pacts can be brokered for financial gain. It happens all the time among knowledgeable magicians. But we recognize that a pact is not going to take us from $10 to $1,000,000 in twenty-four hours. This ties back to the previous point: pacts open back doors and other avenues; they don't break universal laws.

Now, we've covered some of the things pacts won't do, so let's look at some things they do well:

Spiritual ascent: This is perhaps the best form of pact, as the spirits are quick to jump to the aid of aspiring magicians. These pacts can also take the form of initiations in certain traditions.

Wealth: As we mentioned before, pacts won't make you a millionaire overnight, but they can open the doors to feed wealth to you. These can be risky, but the payoff is worth it.

Love: Another risky venture, but one that can be done well with a pact. Certain spirits exist purely for the purpose of creating love, so pacts with these spirits will serve you well in this endeavor.

Baneful Magick: Baneful magick pacts are often a bit dangerous, but with the right spirit, they can be the most potent form of pact possible. Bear in mind, however, that the hot spirits you would deal with for this sort of pact are not exactly the easiest to work with. Use great caution if you go this route.

I think you have a good grasp of pacts, but before we go further, we need to look at the great misconception. Coming back to our second sentence, we always have that little question about the selling of the soul. However, here's the simple truth of the matter: The soul is not a thing that can be sold. It is intricately linked to who you are. You cannot sell your soul any more than you could sell your arm. However, once you look past the literal and into the metaphor, the truth becomes clear. This metaphor is explained here. This was originally a response I gave to someone who begged consistently for me to teach him how to sell his soul to get rich:

"You can devote yourself to an ideal, but you cannot sign rights to your soul over to anyone. You really wanna know how to manifest money with magick, how to 'sell your soul'? I'll tell you. You gotta do it exactly like I did. First, spend half your life studying magick, religion, philosophy, and energy manipulation. You gotta learn what works, and you gotta get good, damn good, until the experts, the masters, the professionals, the best of the best come to YOU for advice. Then, when your head is full, and you can't possibly learn any more, you tell the spirits to show you what else there is to learn. And you keep studying. You study and practice and train until your name is shouted victoriously by your friends and whispered in fear by your enemies. You work until an idle thought would fuck someone's world up, if, that is, you didn't have such impeccable control over your thoughts that you didn't have stray thoughts anymore. Then, when you are confident that you've learned it all, you study more, devouring every piece of information you can, learning from everyone who will teach you. And when you finally reach that pinnacle of mastery, you open a shop, make a name for yourself, and watch the money roll in, because the people know where to go for real magick. You see, you cannot sell your soul to another being. But, you can sell your soul to magick. You give it your all, you live it daily, you love it like you've never loved another mortal, and you dedicate your every breath, every meal, every night's sleep to your art. You love it; it'll love you. And it'll take damn good care of you, if you give your all to it. Sell your soul to magick, and the wealth comes."

The metaphor here is simple: To "sell your soul" simply means to devote your everything to an ideal. Take me, for instance; I have devoted over half of my life to the study and practice of the magickal arts. I live, breathe, and eat magick. I have sold my soul to it, as much as is possible. So don't worry about selling an immaterial concept—worry about where your devotion lies.

And now that we've covered what pacts are, what they aren't for, what they are great for, and the selling of the soul metaphor, we can look at the types of polarities that form within pacts. There are four primary dichotomies within the basic pact, so we will try to make it as clear and concise as possible before exploring the depth of these options. So, without further ado, let us take a look at the different divisions that are possible within typical pacts:

- ○ Long term versus short term
- ○ Single purpose versus multiple purpose
- ○ Specific partner versus general partner
- ○ Physical support versus nonphysical support

Long term versus short term: This division refers to the duration of the pact itself. An example of this type of pact type would be a pact to increase your wealth steadily (long term) or to help you pass an exam (short term.) Each pact has its strengths and weaknesses, and you have to feel out which of these options would work best for your pact when forging it. But all of the polarities fit together, so bear this in mind when drafting your pact.

Single purpose versus multiple purpose: Here, we turn our attention to the goal of the pact. Is this particular deal one that has a single focus, or is it multiple purpose or even open-ended? Examples of these kinds of pacts would be a pact to obtain a certain relic (single purpose), gather certain materials and oversee an operation (multiple purpose), or to assist with general ritual business (open-ended). These particular options sometimes work better with different beings, but we'll get there.

Specific partner versus general partner: This particular dichotomy refers to the object of your pact. Strictly speaking, it refers to whether you wish to name your partner specifically or leave it open-ended for whoever wishes to answer. This is typically not an option considered by many, as most know who they wish to make a pact with. However, as we will observe in the next section, there are times when an open-ended object is a good idea.

Physical support versus nonphysical support: This final aspect refers to your method of payment to the spirits you work with. Most payment is a little of each, but typically one is utilized more than the other in each pact. An example of this dichotomy is to pay for your pact with an offering of incense and blood (physical support) or to pay for it by bringing attention, glory, and honor to the spirit you worked with (nonphysical support). With these four polarities in mind, you can see how your pact can be very versatile.

And now, we turn our attention to the other party in your pact-making process. This is another unfortunate misconception. Many newcomers to the path think that they can only make a pact with Satan, Lucifer, and so on. This is blindingly far from the truth. In fact, a pact can be formed with any spirit you wish! It is imperative, however, to select a spirit appropriate to your goals. It would take longer than we have now to explain every type of spirit in the multiverse, so instead of trying to list every possible spirit, we are instead going to look at some of the most commonly called spirits for pact-making. These are:

Demons: typically preferred for single purpose, short-term pacts, but as with anything in magick this rule is not absolute.

Angels: these are typically preferred for longer-term, more general-purpose pacts.

Ancestors: these can be used for any specialty, depending on who the spirit was in life. But generally speaking, ancestors are great for longer-term work.

Deities: deities are usually versatile, but they really enjoy helping overcome single purposes in exchange for great glory and honor.

Elementals: these can be long or short-term companions, but they are very single-minded. If you feel the need to use these for multiple purposes, it may be better to acquire an elemental familiar.

Animal spirits: you probably weren't expecting this one, eh? These work best for long-term work because typically, if you are making a pact with an animal spirit, it is because you are trying to work with that animal as a totem or power animal.

In addition to these, there are a myriad of other options, such as Yakshini, Lwa, or Orisha, but these are a bit above the level of beginner. For now, suffice to say that when you reach a certain level of skill, they will reveal themselves to you. But let us look a bit more in depth at each of these options:

Demons are arguably the most common pact partners, so much so that many people do not realize that it is even possible to form a pact with other forces. It is, but we will get to that ... Demons are so often called upon because they form such potent pacts. Flip through the *Lemegeton* and read the descriptions of the demons there. They provide a great many benefits, if you can but summon them. A pact takes these benefits a bit further: These demons can be coerced to provide these benefits, and much more, through the use of pacts. The trick is these demons have the minds of lawyers.

Some are benevolent, it is true, many are indifferent, but some are quite malicious. It is in your best interest to not trust in the "good nature" of these beings, and to ensure that your pact is so carefully worded that it cannot be twisted against you. A note, though: This is in no way meant to spread the Judeo-Christian prejudice against demons. All spirits can be this way. However, the reason demons are more like this is simply their nature: They are very close to human. And we as humans always try to twist things to our advantage, so why should we expect any different from the demons?

Angels are a bit less legalistic, as they tend to look at a bigger picture than themselves. This is also why they are preferred for multiple-purpose pacts, as they have the capacity to see how each portion fits with the other and how they can best be made to fit the better interest of their conjurer. Angels do not tend to come to mind when new magicians consider forming pacts, again because of the "pact with a demon" stigma. However, angels are more than willing to enter into an agreement. And they typically only request that you make them known for it, because it is a sad fact that angels are often overlooked in today's mystical culture. Some magicians still keep their flame strong, but this is unfortunately not as large of a group as you may think. In any event, angels are quite useful for pacts, and you would be amazed at exactly what they will do, from love to money to vengeance.

Ancestors are another often-overlooked class of spirit for use with pacts. But even though they are overlooked, there are some traditions that still consider these a vital portion of their initiations. Ancestors are some of the only spirits you can always trust. Consider this: demons may change their mind, deities may remove their favor from you, but your ancestors will always be with you. You are the result of all of their existence, the culmination of many generations of their life's work. They have a vested interest in your success and thus will always be happy to help you.

Keeping that in mind, an ancestral pact could be said to be a mere formality, but it is also a way of showing your devotion and appreciation for their assistance. Additionally, a pact ensures their aid in much more than a subtle, convenient way. However, it also comes with its own price: If you don't maintain your end of the bargain, your ancestors will extract their price. This is always a danger with pact working, but especially so with your ancestors; angering the host of spirits that have nothing but your best interests in mind is asking for trouble.

Deities form fantastic pacts for one primary reason: It doesn't matter what we can offer them; as deities they have everything they need. But, as humans willingly offering adoration and glory, even physical offerings, we are propitiating the very idea of the gods being divine, and this pleases them. Additionally, the gods need us; we are their hands in this world. Offering ourselves in service to the gods in exchange for their aid is an offering they will be most happy to receive. A fine example of a deific pact is my own: I have a pact with the Egyptian god Thoth. He is helping me in the construction of my grimoires, and in return, I am bringing him honor and glory. He was most pleased to accept this pact and has revealed many secrets to me concerning magick and my work.

Another example of this can be found in the book *Necromantic Sorcery* by Dante Abiel. This pact is not explicitly stated, but is implicit in the work that is being done: A powerful pact is formed with the Lords of Death, drawing the necromancer deeper into the current in exchange for their life force. This type of pact is powerful but dangerous. The aspiring magician gives up part of their vitality, even part of their humanity, in exchange for power. But it is also worth it, depending on the pact, and on the magician ... power, after all, carries a high price.

On the other end of the spectrum, we find elementals. For the most part, elementals are not by nature overly powerful, though some are, and they can be made to be. However, as long as a task resides within a certain element's sphere of influence, elementals are ideal for that task. Additionally, elementals form great assistants to the magician, as they are living channels of the elements. It is not uncommon in many traditions for the practitioner to make informal pacts with all four elements, feeding the elements with energy in exchange for a steady stream of elemental assistants. However, elementals are a rather single-minded form of entity, and it behooves the magician to remember this. Elementals are excellent companions and energy channels, but unless you've taken the time to conjure an elemental familiar, it is best to keep your tasks simple.

Animal spirits are the pact partner of choice for aspiring shamans, green witches, and other earth-based magicians. Forming a pact with an animal spirit is a direct way to gain access to the power of the animals to use for your practice. This is similar to the power animal or totem spirit, except that in this case, we approach the animal spirit instead of being approached. There are multiple other benefits to this method as well, because frequently, these spirits will request that as their offerings, you perform some service to Mother Nature, such as cleaning up litter or helping wildlife.

Before we proceed further with the pact-making process, I think a little discourse is in order concerning the hermetic laws and how they relate to pact-making. The reason for this is simple: These laws are the pivotal point of all of magick. Upon these seven principles hinge the entire known mystical universe, so with that in mind, let's have a brief look at them:

○ The principle of mentalism
○ The principle of correspondence
○ The principle of vibration
○ The principle of polarity
○ The principle of rhythm
○ The principle of cause and effect
○ The principle of gender

To take this a little more in depth:

The Principle of Mentalism
The first hermetic law, mentalism, is the most important of the seven. It is this simple foundational principle that forms the basis of the

other seven. Simply stated, this law says that "The all is mind. The universe is mental." This means, in its purest form, that the universe is a thought, a simple mental projection, and it can even be interpreted to mean that we create our universe through our perceptions of it. This statement is the foundation of the idea of "mind over matter." How does this integrate with pact creation? Simple—speaking from a purely psychological standpoint, creating a pact is an excellent way for you to inject your desires into the ether. By handing them over to another entity to assist with or to carry out on your behalf, you also subconsciously relinquish at least a portion of your hold on these desires, which allows the universe to take the wheel.

The Principle of Correspondence

The law of correspondence, in short, states that "As above, so below; as below, so above." This powerful principle is a direct permutation of the first law. A true understanding of this law allows one to create an image of their desires in the ether, and then allows the material world to reflect that image. "Above" here is the astral world, the etheric plane, while "below" is our material universe. What this principle says, then, is that if we create it here, it shall exist there, and if we create it there, it shall exist here. In terms of pact working, this principle is the key to success: The pact is an agreement below to make changes above, and these changes above are then reflected back down below.

The Principle of Vibration

This third law says: "Nothing rests; everything moves; everything vibrates." This particular principle has been verified by science, which confirms that everything is in a constant state of motion. Finessing this particular principle involves a great deal of mental discipline, as well as the application of particular practices. But with its mastery, one has truly obtained the power of the universe. See, this principle relates to the world that everything vibrates. The more material, the lower on the scale, the lower the vibration. The closer to divinity, the higher the vibration. By raising and lowering the vibrations of the self and others, one can literally alter existence. In relation to pact creation, the agreement between spirit and sorcerer to forge a pact together is the setting of intention that emits the vibration of your desire. By striking this bargain, you have stated to the universe that you are truly dedicated to your intent, and you begin to generate the vibration that corresponds to your desire.

The Principle of Polarity

The fourth principle states: "Everything is dual; everything has poles; everything has its pair of opposites; like and unlike are the same; opposites are identical in nature, but different in degree extremes meet; all truths are but half-truths; all paradoxes may be reconciled." This is a powerful principle, as it reveals the truth of so-called opposites. What is revealed in this truth is that in our polarities, such as love and hate, light and darkness, life and death, and so on, these things may be seen as opposites, but are merely varying degrees of the same thing. A knowledgeable practitioner armed with this principle and the appropriate formulas will be able to transmute polarities from one end of the scale to the other, which again forms a permutation of the law of vibration. This principle comes into play with pact working by literally sliding the scale from potential to realization, and it can also be utilized when the pact is to end a habit or finish a project by transmuting the habit into something more positive, or moving the slide from "in progress" to "complete."

The Principle of Rhythm

This law says: "Everything flows, out and in everything has its tides; all things rise and fall; the pendulum-swing manifests in everything; the measure of the swing to the right is the measure of the swing to the left rhythm compensates." This law begins to change direction from our previous principles, as it focuses less on opposites and more on the flow. Simply put, this law states that equilibrium will be maintained by a constant movement toward the center. A fine instance of this is the tendency of a body of high energy finding itself at a low point after a bit, and then returning to a high energy state. This fluctuation in wavelength is easily manipulated by the magician, to employ all kinds of effects. However, a deeper truth is revealed: If you move the center point, the point of equilibrium, either higher or lower upon the scale, the center point of the pendulum swing moves as well. With that in mind, you can simplify a bit of your pact working by simply making a pact that moves your center point. So instead of asking a spirit to deliver $1,000,000 to you, you can ask that your baseline be raised to above your bare minimum necessary. But again, I urge caution—the spirits are tricky.

The Principle of Cause and Effect

Moving in line with our previous principle, this one states that: "Every cause has its effect; every effect has its cause; everything happens according to law; chance is but a name for law not recognized; there are many planes of causation, but nothing escapes the law." In other words, for every action, there is an equal and opposite reaction. Reciprocation is everything in this law. Application of this principle is simple, as it relates more to the practitioner than to a target. If nothing happens by chance, you see, then everything has to happen in accordance with law. And if the practitioner is a master of the law, then the practitioner can easily become a master of the game instead of a pawn, and the utilization of causation will become their everyday practice. In other words, when approaching a task, ask yourself what the effect will be, and what the cause was, of the action you are undertaking. By mastering this discipline, the practitioner literally controls how they influence others, and the possibilities here are endless for what one can accomplish.

The Principle of Gender

At last, we reach the final law, stating: "Gender is in everything; everything has its masculine and feminine principles: gender manifests on all planes." This law speaks to more than just your anatomy, however. This law speaks to the fact that nothing is without balance, and that everything that is generated or regenerated consists of both masculine and feminine energies: light and dark, fire and water, air and earth, and so on. To see how this principle applies to pact working, consider that for every desire you create a pact for, you have to give something up. You have to balance the scales, or else the spirit will not deliver on their end. This forms the circle of give and take, the manifestation of male and female.

Now that we have examined the principles and how they can impact your work, let us move on to the pact-making process. A note here, that it is necessary to be able to perform evocation and invocation to form pacts, which is why this chapter has come after those. If you have skipped ahead, I highly recommend you go back and work your way through those chapters until you are comfortable with them.

The process for forming a pact seems simple, but can be more challenging than it appears. The simplified evocation version is:

Decide upon the purpose, type of pact, and your beneficiary
Research your chosen beneficiary
Draft your pact
Prepare the ritual area

Take authority
Call the spirit and allow it to manifest
Commune with the spirit concerning the pact
Dismiss the spirit
Tie up loose ends

The method of invocation for pact-making is a little simpler:

Decide upon the purpose, type of pact, and your beneficiary
Research your chosen beneficiary
Draft your pact
Prepare the ritual area
Make the call to the spirit and allow it to come down
Commune with the spirit concerning the pact
Release the spirit
Tie up loose ends

We've already covered much of this in previous chapters, but we will look at some specific aspects of the ritual that relate directly to pact-making. Researching your chosen spirit is an invaluable part of this process. This research will give you information on when and how to best conjure the spirit, and if you look hard enough, you can find reports of other people who have worked with this being, which will give you an idea of what to expect. It is also wise to learn the original ritual used to contact the being, as some spirits prefer their original rites. They will likely still answer if you call them through other methods, but they may not be as happy.

While some people like to write their pacts during rituals, I highly advise against this, for the simple fact that you aren't in your normal headspace during a ritual. The spirit holds sway and can influence your writing, and you will be focusing more on the ritual than on your pact. Until you have some experience with pact creation, it is my advice to draft your pact beforehand. Drafting ahead of time allows you to read and review your work, and check it for omissions, loopholes, and errors. Additionally, by preparing a pact ahead of time, you give yourself the opportunity to present it to other magicians and spirits and receive advice on whether or not it is worth going through with.

Once you have your pact written, and you know your spirit well, it's time to prepare the ritual area. The first step to this, as with any high ceremony, is to clean your area thoroughly, and banish any unwanted energies. Once this is done, you can set out candles that are of a color pleasing to the spirit, hang cloths of appropriate colors (or, if possible, tapestries depicting the spirit doing something from its legends—an example of this is to hang a tapestry of Kali standing atop Shiva if you are working with Kali that day), lay out symbolism sacred to the spirit, and so on. Essentially, you are preparing your space for an evocation as with the previous chapter. Once everything is prepared, you can begin to open your ritual. Cast your circle and call your guardians, just as you would for any other ritual.

This is where the formulas begin to differ. If you are performing an evocation, you will be taking spiritual authority over the spirit you are summoning to be able to compel it to appear. However, if you are performing an invocation, then this authority is within the invocation itself. For evocation, you should have determined the proper authority over your chosen spirit during your research phase, though ultimately, all spirits will answer to the force of the divine universe at work. So if all else fails, the universe can be called through the ritual given below.

For invocation, this is your important moment, as you will be calling down the spirit you wish to make a pact with. This is essentially a prayer, calling on the spirit through its virtues and potentially its different names. You are building a connection to this spirit through the first part of this prayer, and then through the second part, once the connection is formed, you are calling this spirit through you and into your ritual space. There are often written invocations, but you can also create your own invocation by paying attention to the spirit's attributes during your research. The connection portion of the invocation is extolling the spirit's attributes, calling on different names, and all around generating their vibration. The first portion of this invocation will be different for each spirit, as it should be direct and personal to that spirit. The second portion, however, is more or less the same.

Once the connection is formed, your next goal is to call the spirit down, into you and your ritual space. This should be a respectful but straightforward statement to the spirit to entice them in. As for whether to evoke or invoke, this is determined by the spirit. Greater spirits such as deities are invoked, while lesser spirits such as demons, angels, and such are evoked. Use your instinct if you aren't sure, as either way, the spirit is likely to answer. Use the below ritual as a guideline, or create one for yourself, if you do not wish to use the original evocation, but the final choice is at your discretion.

Once the spirit has been brought forth, you are at your key moment. With the spirit present, read your pact to them. Put forth your desires, explain your goals, and make your offer. Use divination to determine whether or not the spirit accepts or if changes need to be made. This segment of the ritual is largely free flow, determined by your interaction with the spirit. But, the ultimate goal is to convince the spirit to accept your bargain and to allow you to seal the pact. This is only accomplished during this segment of the ritual and is done by literally allowing the spirit to sign the pact with your hand, or form their seal, or in some other way make a mark upon the paper to seal their involvement.

Once the deal is struck and any offerings are made, it is time for the dismissal or the release. This is essentially the same process whether you invoke or evoke; there is just a difference in your position. If you are performing an invocation, then you simply thank the spirit for its agreement and presence in the ritual, and then you withdraw yourself from the spirit's presence, while also asking it to return to its home. For an evocation, you once more thank the spirit, and then you give it the license to depart: a simple statement that tells the spirit your work is finished, and it is time for it to return to the ether.

Once this is all done, you need to take care of the pact. Some spirits request that it be buried, some ask for it to be burned, but many request that the pact be sealed up, and kept safe. Whatever you have to do, take care of the pact, and then go about fulfilling your end of the bargain. Make your offerings, do your work, whatever it takes to carry your end of the bargain, as the spirits have already begun to carry out theirs.

In the interest of inspiring you for your own rituals, I have devised two sample rituals, one for evocation and one for invocation, for you to use, as well as draw inspiration from. The spirits I select here are for example purposes, though if you happen to use these spirits, you could also use these rituals as they are. These rituals presume that you have already completed steps one, two, and three, and are ready to begin your work.

The Evocation of Bune

Prepare the temple by hanging tapestries or parchment bearing the seal of Bune. Burn incense made of white copal, frankincense, and myrrh, fumigating the temple, and then prepare dragon's blood incense. Lay out a circle for your work, as well as a triangle, in which a parchment with Bune's seal is placed. Place the incense burner holding the dragon's blood on this seal, and light it, allowing a good amount of incense smoke to build above the triangle. Cast your circle to prepare for ritual, and then stand in the center of your circle, facing the triangle, and take authority by the call to the universe:

IO SABOATH!
I call down the divine white light of the universe
to fill me with your power and presence, transmuting
my presence into that of the gods themselves.
By this call, do I make myself the
supreme authority of this space,
and I stand as above all other spirits here,
in my temple, my sacred space.
Here me, all you spirits, and know my word is law.

Now, make the call to Bune:

Bune! Duke of the Hells, ruler of thirty legions!
You who changes the dead, friend of the necromancer!
Giver of answers, bestower of riches, I charge you to come forth!
Answer my call, heed my voice, and appear in my temple!
By your name, mighty Duke Bune, I stir, summon, and
conjure you to appear before me in a form that is pleasing to me,
and without distortion of voice or sight.
Bune, thee I stir, summon, and conjure!
Bune, thee I stir, summon, and conjure!
Tuah-Kulev-Mah-Tin-Neau-Bune!

Repeat the last three lines until Bune makes himself known in your ritual space. Present your pact to him, and divine to determine his acceptance. If he accepts, seal the pact by his sign, thank him, and give the dismissal:

Bune! Thank you for coming to my aid
and for accepting my terms!
May we ever be friends and allies.
As you came in power, go in peace!

Close your ritual and leave the space without looking back.

The Invocation of Kali

Prepare the temple by hanging tapestries or parchment bearing the yantra of Kali, as well as images of her exploits. Burn incense made of white copal, frankincense, and myrrh, fumigating the temple, and then prepare sandalwood and rose incense. Lay out a circle for your work, in which a parchment with Kali's yantra is placed. Place the incense burner holding the sandalwood and rose on this yantra, and light it, allowing a good amount of incense smoke to build above the circle. Cast your circle to prepare for ritual, and then stand in the center of your circle, facing the yantra, and begin the invocation:

Mahakali! Great four-armed goddess of death and time!
You who birthed the universe, the mother of all!
By many names we have called you:
Smasanakalika, Kali, Bhadrakali,
Kapalini, Guhyakali, Mahakali,
Kurukullavirodhini, Kalika, and many more!
You are the keeper of death, the giver of wisdom,
the bringer of enlightenment!
You destroyed the demons of attachment and
paved the way for karma to be removed.
Come to me now, fill me, and fill my temple with your presence.
Hear my plea, Great Mother,
and come down to share this time with me!
AUM HREENG SHREEM KLIM ADYA

KALIKA PARAMESHWARI SWAHA!

Repeat the last line until Mahakali makes herself known in your ritual space. Present your pact to her, and divine to determine her acceptance. If she accepts, seal the pact by her sign, thank her, and give the dismissal:

Mahakali!
Thank you for coming to my aid and for accepting my terms!
May we ever be friends and allies.
Return now to your throne of bone and shadow,
until next we meet!

Close your ritual and leave the space without looking back.

Practical Work

Contemplate what you would form a pact for, and with whom. Do the research and determine whether or not you should perform this pact and how you would go about it. Then, if you are ready, form your pact. Just remember to uphold your end of the bargain.

CHAPTER VII

Spirit Possession

As we have said before, possession is like a deeper stage of invocation. During a possession, the spirit is not simply sharing your body, but rather inhabiting your form entirely. This skill takes some time to develop, even taking many years for some people. But it is a skill worth mastering. The art of possession allows the magician to have a deeper connection to the spirits they work with. Furthermore, possession allows the spirit to have greater control in this plane, and therefore it can effect change in this world with greater ease.

The actual process of possession is similar to the process of invocation; however, there are some differences. The primary difference is the level of contact with the spirit. Invocation is you moving your body with the authority of a spirit within it, while possession is you surrendering your body and allowing the spirit to move it. Bearing this in mind then, it goes without saying that the ability to relinquish control is a prerequisite for the art of possession. This ability can be gained through extensive meditation, invocation, and spirit work in general, as the spirits tend to force you to let go of many things you would not normally release in regular circumstances.

My personal suggestion to take this further is to deepen your immersion phase. When preparing for a possession rite with a new spirit, spend three months of immersion. Every day, spend at least a half hour to an hour meditating with the symbol of the spirit, chanting its name, and allowing its presence to rise around you. Perform invocations daily, acclimating yourself to the spirit being within you. Work your way into the possession rite. This will establish a deep connection to the spirit in question, so that when you are ready to go all the way, it will be easier for you.

When the actual possession rite is to take place, set the stage for the spirit. Dress according to the appearance of the spirit, and have offerings prepared. For instance, if the spirit likes to drink beer, smoke a cigar, and is associated with sandalwood incense, burn copious amounts of incense to fill the area, and have a glass of beer and a lit cigar ready. Meditate with the seal and name of the spirit, and perform the initial invocation. Then, continue to meditate, feeling the spirit within you. At this point, begin to consciously let go of control over your body, as well as any desire or intention for a specific occurrence. Instead, bask in the presence of the spirit, and allow its energy to flow through you.

Continue to call the spirit forth, and invite it to take full control over your body. As this proceeds, allow whatever happens to happen. You may not have much manifestation the first time, but if you've been working with the immersion techniques, it is very likely that you will find your body standing and moving without your conscious permission, or you may even find that you blank, missing a segment of time when the spirit had taken full control. This is the sign of a successful possession, and this state has many uses. For one, the spirit has essentially incarnated on this plane, so it can move through your ritual space and send its energy to whatever goal you have called it for. Additionally, if you are calling this spirit down on the behalf of another, the spirit is now free to commune with them and relay messages directly to them. Here is a sample ritual for a possession rite with the Morrigan:

Prepare a mixture of dragon's blood resin, mugwort, lavender, and rue. Have a glass of red wine ready, and dress in red and black. Draw a large triskele in your ritual room, preferably on the floor and large enough to sit at the center of. Hang an image of the three ravens, or place a bust or statue of the Morrigan where you can gaze at it. Light the incense and allow it to fill your ritual space. Breathe the smoke in and feel its vibration call her forth. Meditate for ten to fifteen minutes on the Morrigan, contemplating how she has presented herself to you during your immersion phase. When you feel connected to her, give the invocation:

Morrigan, mother of the night, the three in one, and yet singular goddess. You rule and reign over the night, and the dead call you Mother. You are the raven that flies above the battlefield, guiding the souls of fallen warriors into the cauldron. You are the mistress of magick, the queen of illusion, the dark mother. Your prowess in battle is unmatched, and those who serve you fear neither blade nor arrow. Hear my call this night and enter my temple. Fill this place with your presence and allow me to feel your heart. Join with me, and allow my hands to be your hands, allow my tongue to be your tongue, and allow my heart to beat with your heart.

Continue to make this call and to chant her name as she rises and settles into your form. When you feel her presence solidly within you, enter meditation again and contemplate her presence. Invite her to take control and chant her name. As you call her, there will come a point that your body rises of its own accord, and drinks the wine. Allow yourself to observe her as she moves about, doing as she will. When she is ready, she will vacate your body. Thank her for her presence and contemplate all that occurred.

You may not always be consciously aware of what goes on during a possession, but the spirits will be aware of your intent and will follow through on your goals. Due to the secrecy of the tradition, I cannot give the specifics of a Lwa possession, but I can give the outline of how the ceremony proceeds. This is different between an open and a personal ceremony, and since this primer is typically aimed at the solitary practitioner, I will give you the outline of the solitary rite.

An immersion phase is not necessary for a practitioner of Vodoun, as their entire life is an immersion phase. When they wish to make contact, they enter their homfort with the intent to make magick. The veve is laid out according to which spirit they are contacting, and then, through ecstatic dance, they work themselves into a trance, fascinating themselves with the veve. Offerings are made, and things appropriate to the spirit are at hand. Then, calls and chants are performed until the spirit seizes the body and they begin to walk about, moving and acting in the ritual setting. Everything that is done is the action of the spirit, working on their behalf. As much as I wish I could go into specifics, I am afraid that is not my role, so that is as far as we will go on that.

But why possession? What makes possession better than evocation or invocation? Aside from the fascination of relinquishing control to a spirit, possession amplifies personal power to an immense level, as your hands are now the hands of the spirits. And, more so than invocation, the spirits can speak in this plane. This moves into the art of channeling as well, for channeling is simply a term used when the term "possession" is not preferred. And in that vein, I will give an exercise my mentor used with me when she taught me to channel.

It should, of course, be stated that when I was learning this skill, I was learning to channel a concept, rather than a living spirit, but the same principles apply. My work began with immersion: I studied the "code" that this principle was based on for months, ingraining it into the fiber of my being. When this was done, we began the meditation work.

Being that this was a principle, rather than a spirit, there was not necessarily an invocation rite to perform. Nevertheless, when we performed our nightly meditations, I recited the code again and again, pulling myself into the current of the principle, until it enveloped me. I allowed it to rise, and then pulled it into myself, and when it was within me, I opened my mouth and willed it to speak.

And my first few experiments were failures. But each time, I grew closer to the truth, until, a month of nightly meditations later, recitation was no longer necessary. I closed my eyes, called this principle forward, and it seized my body and spoke, telling past, present, and future and seeing the hearts of those around me. I learned the value of surrender during these exercises. Surrender to the spirits is difficult but worth it. It is simply a matter of trusting your instincts and letting them say and do as they wish. I cannot put into words the exact process, but I trust that you know what I mean.

A final point on possession: the art of "perfect possession." This is an advanced skill of possession that grants the degree of power in possession, while retaining the consciousness of invocation. This is the ideal state of possession, the true goal of invocation. Those who practice possession seek this state above all others.

The state of perfect possession can be said to be the act of housing two consciousnesses in the same body. In that vein, the first step in gaining the perfect possession state is to house multiple consciousnesses without your intervention. This will create a sort of dissonance within you at first, allowing your own consciousness to peek through and begin to take hold. Of course, this will not be immediate, but as with all other spirit work, it will take work.

To perform your first multiple possession, you will do a few things differently. First, you will divide your ritual area in half, setting half of the stage for one spirit, and half for the other. For your choice of spirits, choose two who work together well. Thor and Odin are excellent choices, as are your ancestral grandparents. Any two spirits, be they ancestral, elemental, angelic, or otherwise, that will work well together are ideal choices for this.

Once your stage is set, you will sit in a place where you can see both spirit settings. Enter a meditation that focuses first on both of these spirits, and then seeing them meld into one as they enter your body. Repeat this meditation several times over the course of fifteen to thirty minutes. After this, begin a blended invocation. This invocation begins addressing each spirit individually, and then blending them together, followed by finally making a single invocation. As this is repeated, the spirits will rise around you.

When these spirits arise, they may come together, or they may come one at a time. Typically, they come together, but either way, you will continue on, inviting them into you by repeating the invocation process and chanting their names. You will feel them take hold, pushing you aside as in a regular possession, but you will also notice a difference: As the two of them rise together, entering your body, their dissonance will allow your consciousness to step in.

This is a difficult state to maintain at first and may only last a few minutes before the spirits return. But with repetition, it can be maintained longer, and as it does, your consciousness will continue to peek through, until you notice that it isn't peeking, but remaining, even with the other spirits with you. When you have achieved this state, you are ready to attempt this with singular possession. Perform your typical possession ritual, but as the spirit rises, allow your consciousness to remain as the spirit rises, communing with it even as it takes hold. This may take some work as well, but you have already begun this, and you will find success with practice.

To give an example of proper multiple possession, here is one sample ritual, calling Saint Michael and Saint Raphael to possess you together.

A Ritual of Possession by Saint Michael and Saint Raphael

Arrange your temple with images of the archangels Saint Michael and Saint Raphael, as you would for a typical ritual. Sit in meditation, focusing on the imagery, seeing the angels blend into your body as a singular entity. When you feel a connection, and it is solid, begin your invocations. First, the invocations individually:

I invoke thee, Saint Michael! Holy archangel of the solar sphere! I call upon thee within thy realm of beauty and majesty!

Michael, mighty, pure, wise, prudent, intelligent, prince of the world, light of the stars, golden and splendorous, Phoebus—shining over the whole world!

Michael, who art high priest of the celestial temple. Mighty general of the heavenly hosts! Celestial guardian angel! You who cast down the fearsome dragon and broke the serpent beneath thy foot! Who sitteth at the right hand of God and weigheth the souls in the scales of truth.

O Michael, when I have called upon you in times of need, you have answered. You have banished darkness from my home, dispelled storms and saved the lives of loved ones. You have been a faithful friend and protector of my family, and have brought honor and glory into our lives. For all of this we thank you!

Come thou forth and partake of these offerings, which we have prepared in thy honor and to the glory of YHVH Eloah v'Daath. May you find them pleasing and empowering. I ask that you offer your blessings to my home and family, and bear our offerings and prayers of thanksgiving to the divine court. We petition thee for strength and protection in all of our undertakings, and that the light of thy wisdom should guide and keep us at all times. In the name of YHVH Eloah v'Daath. Amen."

The universe has an abundance of health, joy, laughter and prosperity to give to me and in vast amounts of abundant supply, and is ready and willing to send it all to me as I AM a child of God and my body is God's divine perfection.

I forgive myself and let go of any and all actions, feelings or thoughts that have created this condition.

I am a master in all that I am and call upon Raphael to invoke the divine blueprint and perfection of my true divine self, God's perfection.

I am ready to live my fullest potential. I am ready to be a light in this world. I am ready to fulfill my mission here on earth.

I am ready to let go of that which has investments in my remaining in an unhealed state as it no longer works for the Master of Life that I AM.

I choose life and the dissolving all my illusions. I retain the original blueprint of my divine perfection that our Creator intended for me.

I choose health. I choose abundance. I choose to fully participate in life. I choose love.

Archangel Raphael, heal me in every way that is needed and anything for which you know needs to be healed at this time.

And so it is, already done. Thank you. Amen.

Then, once these invocations on their own begin to take hold, combine them together into a blended invocation of both angels together:

I invoke thee, Saint Michael! Holy Archangel of the solar sphere! I call upon thee within thy realm of beauty and majesty!

The universe has an abundance of health, joy, laughter and prosperity to give to me and in vast amounts of abundant supply, and is ready and willing to send it all to me as I AM a child of God and my body is God's divine perfection.

Michael, mighty, pure, wise, prudent, intelligent, prince of the world, light of the stars, golden and splendorous, Phoebus—shining over the whole world!

I forgive myself and let go of any and all actions, feelings or thoughts that have created this condition.

I am a master in all that I am and call upon Raphael to invoke the divine blueprint and perfection of my true divine self, God's perfection.

Michael, who art high priest of the celestial temple. Mighty general of the heavenly hosts! Celestial guardian angel! You who cast down the fearsome dragon and broke the serpent beneath thy foot! Who sitteth at the right hand of God and weigheth the souls in the scales of truth.

I am ready to live my fullest potential. I am ready to be a light in this world. I am ready to fulfill my mission here on earth.

I am ready to let go of that which has investments in my remaining in an unhealed state as it no longer works for the Master of Life that I AM.

I choose life and the dissolving all my illusions. I retain the original blueprint of my divine perfection that our Creator intended for me.

O Michael, when I have called upon you in times of need, you have answered. You have banished darkness from my home, dispelled storms and saved the lives of loved ones. You have been a faithful friend and protector of my family, and have brought honor and glory into our lives. For all of this we thank you!

I choose health. I choose abundance. I choose to fully participate in life. I choose love.

Archangel Raphael, heal me in every way that is needed and anything for which you know needs to be healed at this time.

And so it is, already done. Thank you.

Come thou forth and partake of these offerings, which we have prepared in thy honor and to the glory of YHVH Eloah v'Daath. May you find them pleasing and empowering. I ask that you offer your blessings to my home and family, and bear our offerings and prayers of thanksgiving to the divine court. We petition thee for strength and protection in all of our undertakings, and that the light of thy wisdom should guide and keep us at all times. In the name of YHVH Eloah v'Daath. Amen.

Finally, begin the singular invocation of both angels together. This is intended to be a fluid blending of both invocations, but in some, as with this example, it is often better to rewrite the invocations entirely, and so shall we do here:

Saint Michael! Saint Raphael! The Right and Left Hands of YHVH! You are called together in this space to rise with me and dwell here. You are the sword and tongue of God, delivering his message with peace, or with rage. Come now, dwell in this temple I have prepared for you. Come, and dwell! MICHAEL! RAPHAEL!

You will notice this invocation is much shorter. The reason for this is that contact has been made already, and the two have been called together in the blended invocation. Now, what remains is simply to call them into you together, which this final invocation serves to do. Use this final invocation as a mantra to draw them into you.

As contact is made, you will notice the sensations noted before: merging of consciousnesses, and then a dissonance through which you can rise into being. Continue to make use of this in your practice, until it becomes effortless. Once you can use perfect possession, you can not only allow the spirit to work in your world, but you can also watch and learn as the spirit moves. This will prove to be invaluable to you.

Practical Work

Begin formulating a possession incantation for a spirit you are comfortable enough with to work with this process. If you are ready for this step, begin arranging your temple and perform the ritual when everything is set up.

CHAPTER VIII

Familiar Spirits

Now that we have covered the rituals and procedures involved with spirit work, let us move into some more niche topics, which are familiar spirits, spirit keeping, isolated spirits, artificial spirits, and spirit homes. These things are brought up in popular spiritual culture without much being mentioned about them, so we will delve into them here, beginning with familiar spirits.

Read through the *Lemegeton*, and you'll see that many of the seventy-two have the same attribute: "Gives good familiars." But what does this mean? A familiar, as you may or may not know, can be an animal or spirit that serves the sorcerer. What does it take to make a familiar? Not much. Any pet or passing imp can potentially be a familiar. So why do you want a "good familiar"? The answer is simple: because not all familiars are truly capable.

A good familiar casts for the sorcerer in the subtle realms, carries energies to their targets, protects the sorcerer, guides the sorcerer, collects information for the sorcerer, and more. And these Goetia familiars? They are typically skilled in most, if not all, of these areas. That's why so many spirits are known for this in that particular work.

Now, this isn't a universal definition. For instance, in Obeah, a familiar is another term for the "head Bones," so to speak. One of the Bones family, whether it's one we know or one revealed through direct revelation, chooses the sorcerer, and bonds with them to act as their main Bones. But the same functions apply.

So how does one get one of these familiars? There are a variety of methods, which we shall examine here, but the simple list is evocation, invocation, pact creation, spirit creation, and being gifted. Spirit creation will be covered in the next chapter, so we will not look at it here, but we will look at these other methods. Some of the spirits that are ideal for this will be in the glossary, so you may check there if you choose to undertake one of these rituals.

The evocation method is by far the most popular, considering how many spirits in the Lesser Key of Solomon grant good familiars. The process is rather simple: You perform an evocation as usual, and inform the conjured spirit that you wish to receive a familiar from it that fits your needs. These needs may be something that you specify, or they may be the general needs of the sorcerer that you leave to the spirit's discretion. This is up to you, but one thing that will need to be specified is whether this spirit will inhabit a living animal, a body you form, or simply be purely ethereal. Discuss this with the spirit, and ask if it has any preferences. If so, fulfill these requirements; otherwise, be ready with your preferred method. Have a body ready, or have your pet ready. In any event, the spirit will grant you a name and seal to ascribe to your familiar. This will be your method of contact.

Invocation follows much the same principles: Invoke the spirit you wish to work with, and ask for a familiar. In this instance, however, there are not many spirits that are typically invoked that are known for giving good familiars. In this instance, you invoke a spirit whose qualities you wish to work with. For instance, if you work with the vampiric current, you may wish to invoke Lilith and ask her for a familiar. Beyond this difference, the procedure is much the same: discuss your needs, and the form your spirit will take, and be ready with the form for it, as well as to receive the name and seal of your spirit.

The pact-making process follows the same principles as evocation, and can be said to be the same method, except with a document to back the ritual up. This is true in a way, except that with a pact, not only do you receive the familiar, but you specify everything about it, leaving nothing up to the spirit called, and in return, you pay a price, like a rental fee. The terms may include something like a time of service, or a sacrifice made to your beneficiary that is repeated with regularity, or simply dedication. This will be dictated during the formation of the pact.

Finally, we come to the last method of receiving a familiar that will be covered in this chapter: being gifted. This happens when you have served a spirit or deity for a time, and they have seen you as a fitting recipient for a servant of theirs. This often occurs spontaneously, during an invocation or other ritual. The spirit called will take a moment away from your goals, and make it known to you that they are pleased with you, and that they have a gift for you. How they present it to you will depend largely on how you interact with this spirit regularly. Keep your eyes open and be willing to receive whatever gifts they give to you.

Before we look at the possibilities of working with your familiar, I want to look at one more way of gaining a "familiar." I put the term in quotes because, in my mind at least, this form is not a familiar, but a servitor. This is the kind that you seize, either willingly or unwillingly. This is frequently done by necromancers with the shades of the dead, and it can be a powerful tool, but I do not personally advocate this method until you are proficient in spirit work. To that end, I will give no more information on it here, but if you are skilled enough to perform this, you will be able to work the details out on your own. Now, on to the fun.

Familiars can be boosters for magick, messengers, spies, and many other things. Essentially, anything other spirits can be good for, familiars can work toward. However, because of their status as both isolated spirits and lesser spirits, they are best contacted through evocation, at least until a solid enough bond is formed to be able to commune with them without the need for a ritual. This is accomplished through constant work with the spirit, but it will come in time.

Evocation of your familiar is a simple matter, though setting the stage may prove a bit different. My personal recommendation for this is to set the stage in honor of the spirit that granted you your familiar at first, and then as you get to know your familiar, alter the setting to match the familiar directly. You can also use various divination tools, such as the pendulum, tarot, or sangoma bones to determine appropriate elements to work into your ritual.

Another thing you can do with your familiars is work with them in the astral planes. Now, astral projection is not the focus of this work, so I will not belabor the subject, but in case you are not familiar, it is the practice of projecting your consciousness out of the body to traverse the various subtle planes. Getting out of body is simple to explain but difficult to master, as with most other mystical arts, but if you have been doing your meditation, you should have no trouble with it. My favorite method for teaching this technique, I call the talisman method, and it is how I learned. Choose an object to act as your talisman and place it nearby, but out of reach, in relation to where you will meditate. Tell yourself several times that no matter what you do, you cannot move it. Then, enter meditation and visualize the object in your mind's eye. Reach out for it in this visualization and pull. Of course, since it cannot be moved, you will be able to use this as leverage to pull yourself out of your body and to the object. From there, you can explore at will. For more information on astral projection, you will want to do some research and find out what methods suit you most.

Once you are adept at astral projection, you can open an entirely new world of spirit work, but our focus here is working with your familiar spirit, so that is what we will look at. The first thing you should do is call your familiar to you. Let it manifest itself as it will in the planes and take note of how it does so. Also ask any questions to which you need answers, such as what offerings it prefers, any correspondences that help it manifest, and so on. From this point, you should take the time to create an astral space, a sort of pocket dimension if you will, which is arranged specifically for you and your familiar to work together. This may take the form of a temple, a forest grove, a blasted heath, or anything else that suits your needs and desires. Build this space with your familiar, making use of their ability to move easily in the realms to set things up appropriately.

This space will form a jumping off point for any astral work you wish to do with your familiar, so if you are going to do such work, your first stop when you project should be to this space. From here, you can do anything you can do in the physical world, but you can also do things you cannot do here, such as form sharing. This is the act of merging your subtle body with that of the familiar. You can take on their form and travel the realms, seeing them through their eyes. This is also a useful technique for traveling to realms that are otherwise inaccessible through typical astral projection, those that are only accessible to spirits like your familiar. This is similar to the shamanic methods of shapeshifting, through which the shaman can access wisdom and knowledge kept by the animal whose form they are using.

Something else you can do with your familiars is to create a talisman for them, which can serve as an access point to their energy and presence. There are a variety of ways you can do this, but my personal favorite is to make a pendant out of clay. Work with your familiar to discover which herbs and components are sacred to them and work these into a ball of clay. Work this clay into a shape that is pleasing to you and allow it to dry. Once dried, paint the pendant an appropriate color for the familiar and mark it with their name and seal. After this, it is a simple matter to evoke your familiar and request that they empower the talisman with their essence.

One final thing we will look at that you can do with your familiars is send them out to retrieve other spirits. This is really an expansion of evocation but it does have some specific practices associated with it. First, you will need to arrange your temple in such a way as to allow a secondary manifestation area. This is where the constrained spirit will be brought. Second, depending on the nature of the spirit being brought forth, you will need separate offerings and settings to calm the spirit. That being said, this technique is typically used to retrieve stubborn spirits that are troubling the sorcerer, in which case you may also wish to have protective symbols and talismans arranged in such a way as to restrict the spirit from causing harm. Once this is set up, you simply have to evoke your familiar and give them their task. They should be able to perform it quickly, as time is meaningless in the subtle realms, but in case you anticipate difficulties, you can alter your conjuration a bit and instead of telling the familiar to bring the spirit in question back immediately, command them to restrain the spirit and bring them the next time you call them forth, or even to bring them back to you at a set time, so long as you are within your ritual space. This method is easily customizable, depending upon your needs at the time.

Working with familiars is a unique experience among all the forms of spirit work because you are the first to know this spirit, and you get to know it on a level that no one else ever will, and that most never get to know other spirits. You may even choose to take multiple familiars specifically for this purpose. Whatever you do, though, remember one warning: Do not become so obsessed with your familiars that you forget your work. Familiars are but one branch of the great work.

Practical Work

Decide upon the best way to acquire a familiar, and then perform the ritual. Work with your familiar to create an astral space to work within.

CHAPTER IX

Spirit Keeping

Spirit keeping is a fairly new arrival on the occult scene, at least in its current form. But in truth, it has existed for far longer under many different names. At its most basic form, it is the practice of keeping spirits as companions and allies, which is an art that has its roots in ancient shamanic practices, as well as in other spirit-based traditions. However, many modern occultists tend to frown upon the practice for one (or more) of three primary reasons: They consider it an insult to actual spirit work, treating the art of spiritual companionship as a novelty; they see spirit keepers as more Pokémon collectors than actual practitioners; or they see it as a cheapening and commercialization of a sacred art. While their complaints may be valid in some cases, it is not my aim to paint spirit keeping in either a positive or negative light, but rather to shed some light on the subject and answer many of the questions I have received about the practice over the years, so let us do just that.

Before we begin, it is important to note that there is a lot of terminology that floats around the spirit-keeping community, and a lot of it lacks internal consistency. For instance, some groups use the term *entity* for a living being and *spirit* to refer to one that has died. However, I believe much of this is over-defined and borderline pedantic, so for the sake of simplicity, we will not try to sort through those muddled waters. Instead, we will aim for straightforward, simple language.

Spirit keeping is the practice of spiritual entities, typically lesser spirits, being conjured up and "bound" to either a vessel or to the keeper directly. Some refer to this latter form as *body binding*, some refer to it as soul or *spirit binding*, but ultimately, it boils down to the same thing—the "binding" ritual creates a link between the spirit and the keeper, which allows them to commune directly without the need for a vessel. You may be wondering why I put binding in quotation marks, and the answer is simple—binding is a bit of a misnomer. A binding, in occult terms, is a restrictive action, keeping the one being bound from acting in a certain way. Spirit binding, in this context, means something very different, quite the opposite in fact. I personally prefer the term *connection* as it is more accurate, from a mystic standpoint, but since the community at large prefers binding, that is what I will go with.

In the community, there are many different ways to classify the spirits that are conjured and bound, but the most prevalent of these is the arts system, which breaks these beings down into three categories. Spirits that are always benevolent and helpful are referred to as white arts, those that are dangerous and malevolent are referred to as black arts, and those that are neither wholly benevolent nor malevolent, but rather capable of either, are referred to as gray arts. This system can be useful, but the system of dichotomies presented earlier in this work can also be used.

So what sorts of spirits are conjured for these spirit keepers? The short answer is all kinds. As long as a type of spirit exists, and the magician can locate enough of the proper correspondences, they can conjure it. Some of these, such as djinn, demons, angels, and so on, are well-known spirits with specific traditional conjuration methods that are employed in bringing them forth. Others, such as sylphs, dryads, pixies, and so on are less restrictive, and can be called upon with more general-purpose workings. Generally speaking, though, most beings that are conjured and bound in the community are what we would call lesser spirits, and in many cases also fall into the category of isolated spirits, being specifically tied to their keeper. Greater and global spirits can also be conjured, in a way, though in these cases it is less of a binding and more of an empowered connection.

The actual practice of spirit keeping is a largely personal one, with every keeper and conjurer having their own views and practices, but there are some things that are a common thread. Chiefly, having "house rules" for one's collection of spirits is present throughout the community. The rules themselves may change, but there is always a set. The rules act as a kind of pact between keeper and spirit, with the keeper essentially saying that in exchange for spending time with their spirits and giving them gifts and so on, the spirit agrees to uphold the house rules. These rules may include things such as never manifesting in front of family members, not frightening household pets, not disturbing guests, not causing issues with the other spirits of the keep, and so on. Ultimately, they are designed to maintain a peaceful environment and to avoid energetic clashes in the home.

All that said, spirit keeping can prove to be a beneficial practice for the spirit worker, as it has done for centuries. Having a host of spirits to handle a variety of issues has been the cornerstone of many practices, and there is no reason that modern occultists' disdain should be able to change that now. One of the ways that a magician could make use of a collection of conjured spirits is by placing them under the authority of their familiar to assist with carrying out tasks, which brings me to my next major point: the difference between a spirit conjured to be part of a keep and a familiar. The best analogy I have for this is that of buying a car. A conjured spirit is like going to the car lot and picking out the car you like. The car may suit your style, it may have the right features and be your favorite color, and it may be the perfect car for you, but it is still one of many. A familiar is more like custom ordering the car you want, where every feature is up to you and at the end of the day, your car fits you to the letter. To follow this analogy, a servitor is like building your own car from the ground up. Not only do you get to design it, but you also create it, so it is more yours than even a custom order. However, I digress. The point is that companion spirits are a lower class than familiars, but not without merit. Your familiars will be more attuned to your needs and desires than companions, but companions will still be able to work toward goals on your behalf.

However, utility is not the primary reason that spirit keeping has become popular in the modern occult world. This practice is most well known for companionship. Spirit keepers reach out to the spirit world looking for friendship, and there are many spirits that willingly offer it. Developing these sorts of relationships with the spirits yield their own benefits, just as with other forms of spirit work. One of the most common is that these spirits, with a properly developed bond, will act as passive protectors for their keepers, intercepting and redirecting misfortune in the subtle realms before it can cause trouble for the keeper. The inverse is also true: these spirits can draw luck to their keepers without asking, acting as living good luck charms in a way.

Of course, the big question at this point is, how are these beings summoned? Every conjurer has their own methods, developed from their own practice and the traditions of the spirits, but there are some very general methods that can be employed as well. The first and perhaps simplest type of conjuration is the astral summoning. The first step to this is to create an area, like you did with your familiar, in which you can conjure. It is good to do this with your familiar assisting you, as they will already be comfortable with the process. This space should be built into whatever you wish, but it is best that it be arranged as a temple. Inside this astral space, you will want room to work, and you will also want astral emanations of things associated with the spirit in question. When you are ready to begin the process, you will enter this astral space and cast a simple circle. Bring the things you prepared for the conjuration into the circle and lay them out in a way that feels correct, and then focus your will. Focus specifically on the things that you wish for this spirit to be able to accomplish, and what sort of spirit you are searching for. Then, you simply wait. This is a common theme between the different forms of spirit companion conjuration, and it is what makes this sort of spirit work unique: You are not conjuring a specific spirit, but rather putting out a call into the subtle realms, a beacon to draw the desired spirits to you as long as they fit the beacon. When a suitable spirit, or spirits, arrives, you can introduce yourself to them, discuss your needs and desires, and decide whether you will be able to work together. The physical evocation process follows similar guidelines, so I won't belabor that process again.

Once a suitable spirit is chosen, the next phase is the connection or "binding" phase. Again, there are many ways to make this work, but there are some general-purpose methods you can start with and develop as your practice. The idea with the binding ritual is that you are creating a link for the spirit to easily manifest in this world, similar to a spirit house but in a much more diminished version. Following the astral conjuration example, our first binding method will follow that example. Now, it is important to note that the binding does not have to be performed immediately after the con-juration. Some people like to test the spirit a bit before binding, so after the conjuration, they may ask the spirit to work with them for a week or more. If they work well together, then they will proceed to the binding, but if not, then they would be starting over from the conjuration. Once the decision to forge the binding is made, they also need to determine whether this will be a direct binding or a vessel binding. If this is a direct binding, then we may proceed to the binding phase. If it is a vessel binding, then a suitable vessel must be found. Once the vessel is chosen and acquired, we are ready. Enter the astral space and call on the potential companion. If you are using a vessel, call up the astral image of the vessel into the circle. Send energy out to form strands between the spirit and the vessel until a solid bridge is built. If this is a direct binding, then do the same thing, forming a bridge between you and the spirit.

If you are doing this in the physical realm, then you can alter the above method a bit to suit the restrictions of the physical world. However, you can also take it a step further here. For instance, in direct bindings, you can draw the name or sigil of the spirit on your body, or on a vessel for vessel bindings. You can also leave the vessel resting within a circle marked with the name or sigil of the spirit. And, while we are on the subject, in case the spirit does not supply a sigil, you can create one using the instructions in the chapter on created spirits. There are multiple possibilities with companions, conjurations, and bindings, and the only real limitation is your creativity.

Practical Work

Decide whether or not keeping a spirit suits you, and if so, do some research on which spirit or spirits would work best with you. Plan and execute your ritual and be sure to establish house rules.

CHAPTER X

Isolated Spirits

Isolated spirits, as we have previously discussed, are those spirits such as ghosts, dryads, and other spirits that are connected to a specific point in space and time. These spirits are often responsible for hauntings, local legends, and other paranormal phenomena, and as such, are worth discussing as their own topic. There are many spiritual practices that focus specifically on isolated spirits, but one of the most well known is necromancy. We won't be exploring this topic in depth here, but we will discuss some of its practices briefly.

Working with isolated spirits is generally based on building relationships through offerings and spending time in their place of residence. They can be invited to join you in your temple or at home, but that is for later in the relationship. In the beginning, focus simply on building a connection. When it comes to isolated spirits, figuring out what offerings are appropriate is a combination of divination, intuition, and common sense. For instance, when connecting to a dryad, candles probably are not the most ideal choice, but a glass of water would be fantastic.

Another thing worth mentioning here is the philosophy of animism. Animism is characterized by a belief that all things possess a spirit and are, in their own way, alive. This entire practice deals with the concept of isolated spirits, and is a facet of many forms of shamanism and tribal practice. From this perspective, any object can be brought into your practice and treated as a living talisman, as long as it calls to you and is willing to work with you.

So how does one find a spirit to work with? The process always begins with a need: What do you wish to accomplish? There are a number of spirits for a multitude of needs, and research is, as ever, vital in choosing your spirit. For instance, you may wish to take revenge on an enemy, in which case you might be interested in finding a type of fae called a redcap. Or you might have more worldly goals, like wealth, in which case you might be more drawn to a naga spirit. But on a less global scale, you can also consider things like nature spirits. For instance, the spirit of the old oak tree in your backyard would be an excellent choice for health and wealth, while the rose bush in your garden would be great for love.

There are spirits aside from plants, though. For instance, you could work with the spirit of rose quartz for love. The spirit of a bank could be conjured to gain wealth. Even local river spirits can be conjured for a number of purposes, from revenge to protection. But one of my personal favorites, and one of the most well-known classes of isolated spirits, are the spirits of the dead. These can be summoned for a variety of purposes, which are generally based on who they were in life. For instance, a happily married couple can be called upon for love, while a soldier can be summoned for protection or combat, and a lawyer can be conjured for handling legal issues. But this is where research is extremely important, as you don't want to accidentally work with the wrong energy. For instance, a long marriage doesn't always mean a happy one. Research as far as you can, and trust your divination and intuition to guide you the rest of the way.

When it comes to offerings, as I said earlier, trust your intuition, common sense, and divination, but some things are considered standard. If you're dealing with a spirit with specific traditional origins, such as the naga or the fae, there will typically be lore and protocol associated with them that will come out in your research. When it comes to less traditional beings, however, you will have to rely primarily on your big three. Some common offerings include:

- For trees and plant spirits: fresh water, mulch, fertilizer
- For animal spirits: foods associated with the animal, water, animal toys
- For stone spirits: certain oils, light of the full moon, incense, candlelight
- For spirits of place: incense, oils, water, things associated with the place (coins for bank spirits, flowers for spirits of groves, etc.)
- Dead spirits: things they liked in life, white wine, rum, bread, coins

Now, let us presume that you have found a spirit and built a relationship through visitation and offerings. After this, you may wish to make a spirit house as described in a later chapter so that you may bring them home for more streamlined working. As far as working with your spirit, they are similar in function to your familiars, but they are typically stronger than the average familiar. This is due to a number of factors, including the energy fed into them through life itself, as well as through the time and attention fed into them over the years by the people who have seen, cared for, and spent time around their places of origin. For this reason, isolated spirits are often considered to be valuable assets to the spirit worker.

One final note on bringing your isolated spirits home: I mentioned in the last paragraph making spirit houses for your isolated spirits, but this is not entirely necessary in some cases. For instance, if you've found a stone spirit you like to work with, or an animal spirit that you've connected to through their bone, or some other spirit tied to a small object, you can bypass the house entirely and, if they are willing, simply carry the object as a talisman. This talisman can also be further empowered through ritual work, feeding it offerings and letting it rest on your altar. In this way, your spirit can become even stronger and be more capable of assisting with your goals. This talisman can also be used as the central point of a spirit house with a slight alteration: the talisman rests in the spirit house when not in use, charging itself with the energy of the house, and carried on your person when you need its influence with you.

Now, I promised some insight into necromancy, and so I shall deliver. Necromancy is an ancient version of dealing with isolated spirits. The art of necromancy was primarily used for divination, which is honestly a great use for any isolated spirit (they do, after all, see what goes on around them). In order to conjure up the dead, the sorcerer would make their offerings at the grave. They would then use a combination of incantation and intent to bring the spirit to this world. Once the information they were seeking was extracted, they would dismiss the spirit, but they would often take a bit of a reminder with them, a link to the spirit so that they could repeat the conjuration. Most often, this would be grave dirt taken directly from the grave in exchange for a separate offering.

In all honesty, that is all there really is to it at its base level. True necromancy relies only on the relationship between the necromancer and the dead, so if your goal is to work in this path, it is vital to visit the graveyard often and build your relationships. Make offerings at the gate before entering, be respectful and keep proper graveyard etiquette, and most importantly, be patient. The dead do not often rush. Just remember, they are not just tools; they are allies, and should be treated as such.

Practical Work

Get to know your nearby isolated spirits, and start building some relationships. If you happen to run across any isolated spirits that may fill a need in your practice, do the research and start working toward making them your ally.

CHAPTER XI

Created Spirits

One of the most prevalent practices in magick these days is the creation of servitors, thoughtforms, egregores, and other created spirits. This is largely due to the level of control given to created spirits. As a creator, the sorcerer chooses what powers are imbued upon this spirit, how it appears, what domains it rules over, how it is called, and everything else, from the very beginning of the spirit's life. But how do we create a spirit?

This is a simple process, as a spirit can be created by forming an energetic construct and awakening it with your will. The use of artificial spirits has become so commonplace that they have gained a number of titles: artificial elementals, servitors, thralls, thoughtforms, fetches, and so on. However, it is not a recent invention, but rather an ancient art. This practice has existed for centuries and has even become quite famous in certain instances.

One of these instances is the famed Golem of Prague. Essentially, a Rabbi living in Prague received a message from God, telling him that there was a plot to destroy the Jewish community. In his dream state, he received information that led him to create the Golem, a being of clay. He was given life by the holy word EMETH written on his forehead. Supposedly, this Golem went wild and had to be put down. By erasing the E, this word became METH, changing Life to Death in the Jewish language. The rumor is that this Golem is still locked away in a vault, and this story also became part of the inspiration for Mary Shelley's Frankenstein.

On a more personal level, a good friend of mine is proficient in the art of servitor creation, and he once built a servitor with little real point other than to exist. Over time, this friendly servitor went from gathering energy and watching friends to harassing his children and causing nightmares. It got so bad that we wound up locking this spirit inside a box, pouring concrete over it, and burying it in the forest. This brought him to believe a popular misconception concerning created spirits: That when left unchecked, they grow beyond the creator's control.

While this point is valid, it should also be noted that servitors can be left unattended indefinitely, as long as certain parameters are in place. We will cover this more in depth later in this chapter, but for now, suffice to say that as long as your spirit is designed to remain a certain way, it will follow its program.

An odd thing to note is that even though there are hundreds of accurate sources and teachers, most modern occultists would rather use material that is outdated by centuries, created by people with a flawed understanding of what they were doing. This unfortunate truth has been the downfall of many practitioners, and a large portion of my complaints with the internet and the access it gives. However, with the proper understanding, one does not need to rely upon old material, but can instead create a spirit to serve whatever needs fit their situation.

But why take the time to create a spirit when one most likely already exists in the mountains of occult writings that are readily available? There are several reasons for this, some of which are:

Control: With a conjured spirit, your control is limited. But with a created spirit, you have a great amount of control, though not total control. You can design its behavior and personality as you wish.

Detail: You will be hard pressed to find an old grimoire that covers drawing clients to an online website or attracting someone who is as into *Magic: the Gathering* as you are. A servitor, however, can be designed to do exactly that

Artistic Liberty: Some people simply have a gift for creating spirits, and they enjoy using their creations more than older spirits they didn't create.

Just Because: Sometimes there's not really a better reason. But much human progress has been made 'just because we could.'

While this process is as simple or as complex as you make it, here are the basic instructions:

1. Set your goals.
2. Design the appearance of your servant.
3. Create the form.
4. Fill it with appropriate energy.
5. Bring it to life.
6. Let it go to fulfill its purpose.

You should be able to make a spirit right now with these instructions. Set your creative flame alight and let it burn. But, with that in mind, let's look at a more in depth approach. It is my belief that this approach is superior, simply because it gives more of a basis for your construct, and anything with a material foothold can have more permanence than something that is purely energetic.

The first step is to have a Sigil to represent the purpose of the spirit. There are a number of ways to create or receive Sigils. The best Sigils are the ones that appear during meditation, trance, or even astral projection. Following these are those that are granted in dreams or as a response from gods or spirits. Lastly, yet most common, are the kinds of Sigils that are systematically created, such as the letter combinations of Austin Spare or tracing them out upon kameas.

Though I prefer to use sigils that arise through vision, when I do use created sigils, I like to use a planetary kamea related to my purpose. For instance, a Sigil created to call a spirit of war would be created on the Kamea of Mars, while one made to draw wealth would come from the Kamea of Jupiter. There are numerous other grids, however, and you can even create one yourself if you so wish.

To begin, choose a word, phrase, or sentence to sigilize. If you are doing this with more than one word, then use the Spare method to reduce the letters. Eliminate repeating letters, combine letters that fit together, and eliminate vowels if you wish. I personally do not remove the vowels, but that is your choice. When you have your letters, convert them to numbers if you are using a Kamea, or leave them as letters if you are using a letter grid.

To convert your letters into numbers, array the alphabet against the numbers in the Kamea. If your Kamea is one through nine, repeat the alphabet every nine numbers. If it is thirteen, repeat them every thirteen. If the grid is more than twenty six, simply line the letters against the numbers in ascending order until you run out. Once you have your numbers, or if you are using a letter grid, trace an appropriate symbol, such as a triangle, circle, or square, over the first letter or number. Extend the line to the next character of the sequence, and continue on until the end. At the end, draw a trident, perpendicular line, or other appropriate symbol. Once the main Sigil is made, you can make other Sigils to represent rules, parameters, and other things you want included. These will include things such as where it draws its energy, what it can and cannot do, and other such instructions. You will also include rules concerning personality, behavior, and so on.

Once you have your Sigils, create a talisman out of them. This can be done with paper, clay, wood, metal, and such. The more permanent you wish your servitor to be, the more solid your material base should be. This will be your link to your spirit for conjuring, feeding, or destroying it. You may also consider making a statue of the being. Or, you could make a servitor to match the statue. You should also remember that some things, such as spiritual statuary, may already have a presence on them.

Cleanse these sorts of things, or else avoid them altogether. Just remember to empower the materials you are working with, and to allow them to be true conductors of energy rather than dead materials. My personal favorite for this is to use oven bake clay. If I choose to allow the spirit to live on, I will solidify it. Otherwise, I can dismantle it easily.

If you are not making the servitor to match the statue, then they can take any size and shape you can imagine. Of course, form should follow function. If you are designing a servitor for intelligence work, something like a flying security camera would be ideal. If it is an attack servitor, model it after a warrior. The possibilities are truly limitless.

For generating the psychic form, the body as it were, you will need to meditate with your physical form and your seals. Feed them energy, and allow them to take form. Allow the seals to come together and form a singular form, solidifying into a body. Feed this image energy, make offerings to it and grant it your power. This is a simple exercise. You can also do this with multiple participants, each feeding your servitor, but if you do this, everyone in the ritual should have a clear idea of what they are doing, otherwise conflicting ideas will cause your servitor to collapse.

You can use specific energies, such as those from planets or stars, or the elements. In fact, using elemental energy has given rise to the concept of creating artificial elementals. You can also use all four elements to create a body, following the old alchemical principles. Personally, I prefer to keep a single element for simple servitors, and to use appropriate combinations for advanced servitors. For instance, if my servitor is intended to be for influencing emotions, I will blend air (to bend the mind) and water (to manipulate emotions). Whatever you choose, be sure to follow the simple principle: Form follows function.

After you have formed the body and empowered it, it is time to bring it to life, by applying your will and delivering it. Two of my favorite methods are to breathe life into the material basis to deliver the Breath of Life, and pointing my wand at the material and calling out its name, commanding it to come alive. Either way, once it lives, you should tell it what you want it to do and send it on its way.

Most people look at these servitors as computer programs, but I don't see this as the case. Once they are brought to life, they are constantly learning and growing, drawing in energy. This is especially true of long term servitors, as these are often designed to grow and adapt. However, in doing so, I recommend that you create a special parameter seal defining you as the master of the servitor.

Finally, it is usually a good idea to give your creations a date to dissolve into formlessness, unless your servitor is meant to be indefinite, or at least long term. It is best to tie this to a specific event, such as an accomplishment of your task, rather than just a day, to keep your magick from being canceled by an abrupt ending. Some people claim that any servitor left alone will turn wild and need to be destroyed. This goes back to the problem my friend had with his servitor gone wild. This is certainly a possibility, but it isn't likely. His spirit had no purpose, other than to see if he could. If you have given your spirit a firm purpose, you should not have this problem, even if your servitor roams free for years. I personally keep several created thralls, and all of them, though they have grown and changed, have retained their base purpose and not gone wild. This is because their purpose was set in stone and established, as was their submission to me as their creator.

Practical Work

Design and create a servitor and set it to its purpose. Keep an eye on it to ensure that it is functioning properly.

CHAPTER XII

Spirit Houses

This is our final chapter that concerns traditional spirit conjuration, and is one of my most favorite topics in all of spirit work. We will be covering spirit houses, with a special focus on my favorite kind of house, the spirit bottle. Bottles have always held a special place in magick, and especially in the NOLA Voodoo, Haitian Vodoun, and American Conjure communities, and they have a special place in my heart. Really, anything can be used as a spirit home, and technically, poppets, statuary, and even Gris Gris bags are spirit homes. But there is something simply magickal about bottles.

All over the world, humans have found a way to create physical places for non physical beings to reside. This can be seen in the ancestor bottles of Hoodoo, the Djabs of Vodou, and the Brass Vessel of the Goetia. These have served three main purposes:

- ° To allow us an easy point of contact with the spirit in question
- ° To allow them an easy point of contact with us
- ° To imprison dangerous spirits, or restrict their contact.

While anything with any level of spiritual potency can be used to house a spirit, there are some things that are better than others, whether due to the level of spiritual essence, the components of the house itself, or the direction of the spirit itself. When selecting a home, use a combination of research, intuition, and divination to determine the best choice. You may have also noticed a lack of information on this topic in the common writings you will find. This is due to a simple fact: This is an advanced art, something beginners shouldn't play with until they are ready. There are two reasons for this. The first is simply good business, you do not want to give away the process by which you make money, and this method is extremely lucrative for Houngans, Bokors, and Mambos, among many others. The second is that this particular skill is easily misused. Many times, a magician will create a home for a spirit, only to find that the cost outweighs the value. This is especially true when tourists by Vodou bottles from unscrupulous Houngans and Bokors, which turn out to be windows into the client's world for the spirit to wreak havoc when it isn't pleased.

While certain spirits can be very beneficial to have around, it can be devastating if you choose the wrong spirit. The stories that come out of these unfortunate relationships may bring to mind stories of haunted houses, but it is even worse, as the haunting is tied to the magician and the spirit home, not a specific location. The horror stories of these instances are more common than you would think, though they are largely misinterpreted.

For instance, the first spirit bottle I ever made for a client was for Aphrodite. My client requested that she bring him the love of his life. The cost was not high: A rose every full moon. However, my client gave one rose, and believed that should be all. This did not please Aphrodite. Further, my client then gave the bottle away as a trinket. Aphrodite cursed him. At the time of this writing, that was nine years ago, and to this day, he is still alone.

So as you can see, there are some techniques, such as this one, that should not be used by beginners, as without proper experience they can be dangerous. Even experienced magicians, such as myself, have run into problems. I personally had a problem with a rather demanding spirit I had made a bottle for from the graveyard. She became unruly and demanding, and wouldn't do her work, so I released her and disassembled the bottle. When this happens, be ready for a fight. The spirit has made their home, and they are often loathe to leave it.

The first thing you need to know about the spirit you are working with is whether it is isolated or global. We have covered this before, but it takes a different meaning when dealing with spirit houses. You can bind a global spirit in a spirit house, but this does not change the nature of the spirit. It would be impossible for anyone living today to so completely lock away the essence of Hades, for instance, that no one else would be able to contact him again. Bottles made for beings like this should be taken less as containing the whole essence of the spirit, and more as being a direct line to their power.

Isolated spirits are a bit different. If you catch one of those in a house, then they are bound. As they can be pinpointed to a single space, they are much easier to lock up. It is for this reason that bottles, pots, lamps, and other items are often used to trap dangerous spirits that are causing issues for other in their homes.

When you create a spirit bottle or other home with these spirits, it can either act as a permanent home for them, a point from which they can be easily conjured, or a prison. We will discuss the nature of imprisonment later, but I warn you, this act should be a last resort, after attempts at banishment and exorcism have failed. Imprisoning a spirit creates a potential danger that could at any time be unleashed upon you if someone manages to undo the binding, or if the vessel is destroyed somehow.

From here on out, I will be referring specifically to spirit bottles. However, these instructions can be applied to any container, such as boxes, pots, jars, and so on. I like bottles because they are pretty, portable, and come in many shapes and sizes. But I digress, let us look at the material for your spirit bottle. These are: The connection to the spirit, which we shall call the material soul; the staging materials, which will be a smaller form of the stage that is set during evocation as well as any offerings you make to the spirit; and the tools and equipment it will use.

The material soul is perhaps the most important aspect of any spirit house, as it is your connection to the spirit, which serves to anchor it into the vessel. It could be graveyard dirt or a bone if this is for a spirit of the dead, a collar or favored toy if this is for a lost pet, or a Grimoire seal, picture, or statue if it is appropriate to the spirit. Whatever you choose, it must be something intrinsically linked to the spirit, so that you have the most solid connection possible.

Sometimes, you may have to go a little out of the way to get a material soul, and sometimes, it may be unconventional. I have been forced to make bottles for beings with no seals associated with them, only names and associations. From these, I have created sigils based on their names, and wrapped these around satchels created from their correspondences. For instance, with the Morrigan, I would fill a black satchel with grain, a few drops of blood, and a raven feather, and feed the satchel with dark beer and red wine. With a combination of intuition and creativity, things like this are simple to put together.

In the beginning of this book, we discussed preparing your temple in such a way as to be conducive to the spirit you are conjuring, so that they may be comfortable manifesting. You need to do this with spirit bottles as well. The color and decorations on the bottle are obviously important. If you are using the Sigil as a material soul, you can draw this all over the outside of the bottle. You can also add grave dirt for dealing with the dead, vibhuti powder and sandalwood for Nagas, and so on.

After setting the stage for the spirit, you may also want to link this to your own temple. Dirt is ideal for this, mostly. Dirt from your home, your job, the bank, your kids school, and so on. The idea is that you are blending the world of the spirit with your own. This gives them a major foothold in your life, though, so take this step with care.

In addition to setting the stage for your spirit, you will also want to include offerings to the spirit to entice them in. This can be things like candles, incense, food, drink, and so on. The idea is that they will see their home made how they liked it, and your offerings, and be more than willing to enter it.

After you have set the environment, provide some tools for the spirit to use. These can be herbs and other items used in formulas for the type of magick you want the spirit to perform, or they can be literal tools that help connect the influence of the spirit to the physical world. It is important to note that not all of the items need to go inside the bottle. They can be fixed to the outside if necessary, such as when I fixed a beautiful necklace to the outside of a bottle made to seduce a beautiful woman.

One ancient type of spirit house actually gives the spirit, another spirit. Apart from the material soul in the home, they will include links to certain spirits that serve as assistants. A prime example of this is including the bones of a rat, so that the rat may get places that the main spirit cannot and act as an intelligence agent. This is also seen in certain Puja altars in the Aghori tradition: Aside from the deity that dwells there, Nagas will be brought in to serve that spirit.

The last step is getting the spirit to move in. Typically, this is nothing more than an evocation of the spirit, and then asking it to dwell in the bottle. This depends on the spirit you are dealing with, of course. But ultimately, either the spirit will consent, or it won't. There is no guaranteed ritual that will get the spirit to agree, unless we are talking about imprisoning the spirit, which we will look at here.

When it comes to imprisoning the spirit, I have a particular method that I like to use. The material soul is still necessary, as you need a way to link the spirit into the bottle. However, the stage is always the same. Choose a black bottle, or paint a bottle black. Paint the four pentagrams of the Lesser Banishing Ritual outside of it. Upright Pentagrams, one in red, one in yellow, one in blue, and one in green. Inside the bottle, place a mixture of frankincense, myrrh, and coriander, an iron chain, a raccoon paw or the bones of a raccoon, and a piece of hematite.

When this is gathered, call the spirit by whatever method you can. When it is present, perform the Lesser Banishing Ritual of the Pentagram, but instead of banishing outward, banish inwards, driving the spirit into the bottle. When the spirit is inside, seal the bottle closed, light a black candle over it, and wrap an iron chain around it, placing a lock upon it. You may do with this bottle what you wish, but I recommend keeping it safe. If the spirit is released, it may seek vengeance. This method works for both isolated and global spirits, but remember, with a global spirit, you are only binding your interaction with the spirit, not the entire spirit.

Of course, I want to mention again that bottles are not the only type of spirit home. Anything can be a home if you are creative enough. Consider using a statue of Saint Michael, draped with offerings and appropriate staging materials, with daggers and shields given to him to protect you. Or, a poppet, made with a material soul of your target woven inside to cause them to truly live inside. Or the dreaded Mummy hex, which uses these principles to trap the shadow of your target. As with much in magick, you are limited by only your imagination.

Practical Work

Decide whether or not a spirit bottle is appropriate for your work, and if so, do the research and start gathering your materials. When everything is collected, do the ritual work and give your spirit its new home.

CHAPTER XIII

Spiritual Self-Defense and Cleanup

As we approach the end of this work, we must touch on the final aspect of spirit working: the cleanup. Sometimes, we have negative attachments that try to follow us home, invade our rituals, and otherwise make our ritual work difficult. Sometimes, they aren't negative attachments at all, but spirits that came for the offering and didn't want to leave after they were dismissed. And sometimes, they are exactly the spirits we wanted, but for whatever reason, they wanted to stay long after their work should have been completed. In these instances, we must turn to our toolbox of spirit removal options.

That said, ideally, we have other avenues open to us as well to prevent the need for spiritual removal. So we will cover these self-defense methods first, and then we will turn to removal. As with most forms of magick and ritual, there are levels to spiritual cleanup, which we will cover in turn.

First up in the realm of self-defense, we have the use of talismans. Talismans and amulets have been used for many purposes throughout the years, but protection is high on the list. Many grim-oires even make mention of wearing talismans and sigils to ward off spiritual attack. These talismans can take many forms, from simple to complex. Crystals are one form of simple talisman. Hematite makes an excellent stone for protection, as it grounds out excess energy. Another good choice is onyx, which has natural general protection qualities. Another method is to carve a Thurisaz rune into a pendant made of oak wood. The combination of energies forms a powerful protection talisman. Hamsa hands and evil eyes are also commonly used items.

One particular form of talisman that is particularly potent, and extremely versatile, is the pentacles of Solomon. There are forty-four of these, and they correspond to the seven planets. While these pen-tacles have many purposes, there are some that deal specifically with both spirit work and protection. Pentacles to be used for protection would be the Fifth Pentacle of Saturn, the Second, Third, Fourth, and Fifth Pentacles of the Moon, the Sixth Pentacle of Mars, and the Third and Sixth Pentacles of Jupiter. If you wish to wear a pentacle to amplify spirit work, these would be the ideal choices: the Fourth and Fifth Pentacles of the Sun, the Third Pentacle of Saturn, and the Fifth Pentacle of Mars. You may also use these in tandem with each other to amplify your own energy.

Another method of spiritual self-defense you may employ is to call upon your guardians. We mention this in the chapter on offer-ings, that you should make your offerings to them first so that they would cover you from the other spirits. You can take this a step further, however, by performing an entire ritual to them first. Make offerings to them and draw your circle, calling forth your guardians and protectors. Ask them to bless and protect you as you move forward with your other ritual work. You may wish to use some form of divination to confirm with them that they accepted your offerings, but you can also simply wish to trust them.

If you are performing rituals in your sacred space, you may wish to use a more permanent form of protection. There are many ways to do this, but my personal favorite is the use of sigils. You may wish to do this by hanging pictures or banners, or by drawing them directly onto the wall. I personally use this method. In my temple, I have used cascarilla chalk to draw witch's knots, pentacles, incantations, and a few other more personal things on the walls. These are empowered every time I perform ritual work by feeding them with Florida water, incense, and energy. Another technique that is often used is the setting of mirrors. Many people will set a mirror at every door and window, or they will stand windows up around the building at each wall. Either way, the reflective side is set out to repel unwanted energies. You may also choose to amplify this through the use of symbols, but this is not entirely necessary. Finally, some choose to bury stakes at the corners of the space. These can be iron railroad spikes, nails, or even carved wooden stakes. The idea behind this is that you are setting a boundary with fierce objects, which will repel spirits through the threat of violence.

Now, when it comes to spiritual cleanup, there are some things that should be a part of a regular practice cycle and some things that should be employed in only special cases. Smoke cleansing and water cleansing should be used fairly regularly to clear up energetic buildup, while banishing and exorcism should be reserved only for times when they are necessary, such as when a spirit will not leave after an offering or when the wrong spirit answers a summons.

Before we dive into smoke cleansing, it is important to make a note about smudging and sage: Just because you burn white sage and wave it around with a feather and shell does not mean you are smudging. The act of smudging is a very specific cultural practice, which is done in a specific way. If you are not initiated and trained, you are not smudging. And that is perfectly fine. Smoke cleansing can be done by anyone, and it can be used with prayers and incantations of your own, if you desire, and it is just as effective.

Now, smoke cleansing is a simple cleansing method which, as its name implies, employs the use of herbal smokes to cleanse an area, as well as to draw in vibrations that you want to have in your space. Some herbs you can use for this include cedar, to remove negative energies and encourage the flow of pure, positive energies; yerba santa, to cleanse the area of heartbreak vibes and draw new love; juniper, to banish sadness and encourage happiness; and pine needles, which specifically target negative spirits and send them away, sealing the space between them. Sage, of course, is common, but if you so choose to use sage, either use blue sage, which is not in as much danger of extinction as white sage, or white sage that is ethically sourced from the Native tribes that raise it. But avoid commercialized white sage, as these companies are harvesting and selling it into extinction, and that is not the energy you want involved in your practice.

Having selected your herb, or herbs, the process is simple. If you have acquired your herbs that are already in stick form, then you are ready to go. If not, you may burn them as is, or you can make them into a stick. All you have to do is gather your herbs into a stick, and if you would like, you may braid them. Then you'll want to tie your herbs in a semi-tight stick with hemp cord. Whatever you choose to do, you will want to place your herbs on a shell or plate and light them on fire. Let them burn for a few moments, then gently blow them out. Wave the smoke throughout your space, with either a feather or your hand. As you scatter the smoke through the space, visualize the smoke driving out negative, stagnant energy and drawing in positive energy. You may also use the smoke to cleanse yourself by waving the smoke over your body.

Another personal favorite is asperging, or liquid cleansing. Florida water is the most popular form of this, and it is not overly difficult to make. In order to make your own Florida water, add the following to one pint of distilled spring water: two ounces of vodka, six drops of bergamot oil, fifteen drops of cinnamon oil, three drops of clove oil, two drops of lavender oil, and twenty drops of lemon oil. You may also wish to add some of the dried or fresh herbs to the formula to give it some color. Shake well and store in a cool, dry environment. You can also use a citrus asperge, which I personally prefer. Add nine drops of lemon essential oil and nine drops of orange essential oil to one gallon of distilled spring water. Shake this well, and store in a cool, dry environment. Once your asperge is made, it is simple to use. Some people like to put it into a spray bottle and spritz it around the space. Others like to splash it around right from the bottle. Either way, as you do so, visualize the water washing away negative energies, leaving the space clean and clear.

Now, while these practices are good for general-purpose cleansing, sometimes you have to step up the intensity. But in order to determine whether or not this is necessary, there are two tests I will make use of. The first of these is what I call the lemon detector. In order to use this technique, you will need a few lemons and plates. Set plates out in various locations and place the lemons on them. Some, you will want in places you go to frequently, such as your bedroom, while others will want to be in places that you do not go often, such as in the shed out back. Then, you will want to monitor them. You don't have to check on them daily, but every few days is sufficient. Lemons, being organic things, will rot eventually. However, if you have an attachment on you, the lemons you are around more frequently will rot more quickly.

A second method you can use is the egg test. This is sometimes called limpia, but again, limpia is a specific practice. The egg test is simple, requiring only a fresh egg and a glass of water. To perform this test, roll the egg gently over your entire body, from the top of your head to the bottom of your feet. Alternatively, you can gently pass the egg a few inches above your body, close enough to touch your aura, but far enough that it is not making direct physical contact with you. While doing this, focus your intentions on the egg absorbing any negativity you have around you. When you have passed the egg completely over yourself, crack the egg into the glass of water. Give it a moment to settle and then study it. The egg will form patterns in the water. There is no set pattern, but it can be generally accepted that if the water forms a negative pattern, such as a skull, spider web, claws, and so on, then it has detected a negative attachment.

If your tests reveal an attachment, you have four options. The first is to perform the cleansings mentioned earlier on yourself and hope that is enough. You can perform the tests again to determine if it is, or trust your intuition and divination. If it is not, you can take option two, which is a cleansing bath. Baths are a powerful method that have been used for years as a way to soak yourself in the energy you wish to attract, or to wash away the energy you don't need attached to you. There are many bath formulas, but my personal favorite is very simple. Bring a gallon of distilled spring water to a gentle boil and add into the water half a cup of rosemary, quarter of a cup of bay leaves, quarter of a cup of white clover blossoms, and quarter of a cup of eucalyptus. Let it simmer for about ten minutes, then strain the herbs out and add the liquid to your bathwater. Soak in this formula for about twenty minutes, gently wiping yourself down with the water while visualizing the water wiping away any negative energy and attachments. After this is done, step out and dry yourself. It is recommended to perform another test to see how effective the bath was.

In the event that neither cleansings nor a bath were able to remove the attachment, it is time to turn up the heat with a banishment. There are many forms of banishment, but my personal favorite is the Lesser Banishing Ritual of the Pentagram. This is not the most powerful banishing ritual in the world, but it is generally effective for most things you will encounter, and if it is not, then you are likely at a point where you know a more effective method.

Take your athame in your right hand or use your index finger. Face EAST. Perform the Qabalistic Cross as follows:

Imagine, at the first word intoned, a brilliant white light descending from above. Touch the forehead and vibrate *ATEH* (thou art). Imagine that same brilliant white light form a six-inch diameter sphere just above the crown of your head. Touch the middle of the solar plexus and vibrate *MALKUTH* (kingdom). Imagine a shaft of light descending from the crown sphere and to the feet where another six-inch sphere expands just under your feet. Touch the right shoulder and vibrate *VE-GEVURAH* (and power). Imagine a six-inch sphere of brilliant white light appear just next to the right shoulder. Touch the left shoulder and vibrate *VE-GEDULAH* (and glory). Imagine a shaft of light emerging from the right sphere and cross your breast to expand and form another sphere at your left shoulder. Clasp the hands before you and vibrate *LE-OLAHM* (forever).

At this point imagine clearly the cross of light as it extends through your body. Hands as before, with the dagger between fingers, point up, vibrate AMEN.

Note: Any image or figure traced in the air with the finger, dagger or another magickal instrument, is to be imagined in brilliant glowing white light. In more advanced working, other colors may be used. Make sure that all images drawn are correct, as brilliant as possible, and complete. The beginning and end of a drawn pentagram must come completely together.

Draw, in the air facing EAST, a banishing earth pentagram, which begins at the bottom left point as you see it and moves clockwise, and, bringing the point of the dagger to the center of the pentagram, vibrate the name *YHVH* (pronounced YAHD HEY VAU HEY). Without moving the dagger in any other direction, trace a semicircle before you as you turn toward the SOUTH. Again trace the pentagram, bring the dagger to the center of it, and vibrate the name *ADNI*, (pronounced AH-DOH-NEYE). Again, trace the semicircle with the dagger to the WEST, trace the pentagram, bringing the dagger to the center, and vibrate the name *AHIH*, (pronounced EH-YEH). Then, turn toward the NORTH, while tracing the circle, trace the pentagram, bring the point of the dagger to the center and vibrate the name *AGLA*, (pronounced either AH-GAH-LAH or ATAH GIBOR LE-OLAHM ADONAI). Return to the EAST, completing tracing the circle of brilliant white light, bringing the dagger point to the center of the EAST pentagram.

Extend the arms in the form of a cross, say: *BEFORE ME RAPHAEL* (pronounced RAH-PHYE-EHL). Imagine a brilliant white archangel in front of you and facing you. In his/her right hand is a magickal sword held with the point upright. The background is a pale, pure, bright yellow. Cherubs can be imagined near the archangel. Imagine a gentle, refreshing breeze, cleansing and purifying the air. Then, say: *BEHIND ME GABRIEL* (pronounced GAH-BREE-EHL). Imagine a brilliant white archangel behind you and facing you, holding in their right hand an exquisite silver chalice. He/she is standing on a cerulean-blue ocean and dolphins or mermaids are nearby. Imagine feeling the mist and cool spray of the ocean breeze. Then, say: *AT MY RIGHT HAND MICHAEL* (pronounced MEE-CHYE-EHL). Imagine a brilliant white archangel at your right, facing you, and holding in their right hand a transparent scarlet red wand with a scintillate pure diamond top. Waves of scarlet, red-orange and orange fire in the background. Imagine you feel the heat and power emanating from the SOUTH. Then, say: *AT MY LEFT HAND AURIEL* (pronounced AWE-REE-EHL). Imagine a brilliant white archangel at your left, facing you, and holding between their hands a disk with a white pentagram in the center. The ground is russet brown, the leaves of the trees are olive green, there are black shadows from the trees in a number of places, and the light is citrine (light yellow-green.) Feel the solidity of the earth, and imagine the odor of the leaves and muskiness of the ground.

Now, say: *ABOUT ME FLAMES THE PENTAGRAMS, AND IN THE COLUMN SHINES THE SIX-RAYED STAR.* Imagine the complete circle of brilliant white light at whose quadrants are the four pentagrams. At the center is the Qabalistic Cross of Light extended through one's body. Repeat the Qabalistic Cross, and stamp your right foot at the conclusion of the complete operation.

And that concludes the Lesser Banishing Ritual of the Pentagram. You will find that it is quite potent and can help handle a great many things by itself. Feel free to research it and to alter it to fit your traditions if you wish, so long as the replacement ritual is fluid.

Now, the Lesser Banishing Ritual should handle most things you will encounter. However, in the event that it cannot, whether it is because you are being attacked or are experiencing a very deep attachment, the next step up is the exorcism. There are many ways to do this, but they all require authority of some sort. You can do this through invocation of a deity, or by invoking the universe itself. What is presented here is a formula of my own design, proven to be quite effective, that draws upon the authority of the universe itself to drive out unwanted forces. However, if you so wish, you may make some alterations to the formula to fit whatever deity you wish to draw upon.

First, you will want to consecrate some Florida water. To do this, set a bottle of Florida water on your altar and place your hands upon it. Close your eyes and focus on sending energy into the water. As you do this, visualize the light of the universe itself flowing through you to purify the water. If you wish, speak a prayer or incantation to seal this act. To finalize the working, leave the water outside under the light of the full moon overnight. Collect the water in the morning and you're ready to move forward.

Gently rub some of the water onto yourself and spread it around the area where you will be performing the exorcism. This begins the process by spreading the consecrated energy of the universe around, building the charge that you will amplify through ritual. When you are ready for the ritual itself, gather together two white candles and incense made from frankincense and myrrh. Open your ritual circle as normal and perform an offering to your guardians and protectors. I would recommend a major offering, but follow your instincts. When the offering is complete, light your incense and allow the smoke to suffuse the air. Light your white candles and set them at either side of your ritual space. When you are ready, begin the incantation:

> *Light of the universe!*
> *Divine essence that quickens and empowers all things!*
> *Hear my call, and shine your light upon me!*
> *Fill this vessel with your strength*
> *and fill this space with your grace!*
> *By earth and sea, by flame and sky, let us move and act as one!*
> *May my arms be yours, may my voice be yours,*
> *and may my eyes see your light!*
> *Come and let us be united!*

As you do this, visualize the divine light pouring into you, making you into a living emanation of the divine. After the incantation is completed, allow a few minutes for the energy to settle. Then turn your attention to the ritual space. Hold your hands out to your sides at shoulder height with palms out, and visualize the divine light exploding out of you in pulses. As you do this, speak this incantation:

Divine light, let all things that are not
in alignment with my highest good burn away in your light!
All spirits, energies, and essences that are not in my service
be driven away before the all-consuming flame of the Divine!
Hear me, all you dark beings! I command you to be gone!
My voice is divine, and my call is irrefutable!
Go, be driven out before the divine light!
Leave this space, and do not return without invitation!

Hold this position for several minutes, as long as it takes for the light to stop pulsing and to burn away the negative attachments. When the ritual feels complete, lower your arms and speak one final incantation:

Divine light, I thank you for your gifts and blessings!
I ask only that your light continue to protect me
and drive away all those things
that do not serve my best interests.
Thank you again, and let us remain allies!

Walk away from your ritual space, allowing the candles to burn out on their own. This particular exorcism is not overly complex, but it generates immense power quickly. If you choose to substitute the universe with a deity, feel free to expand upon the incantations and offerings to suit your deity more appropriately. These tools will serve you well, and they will grow and change with you as you expand your practice.

Practical Work

Begin practicing regular cleansings, and spend some time learning how to perform the Lesser Banishing Ritual of the Pentagram. These things will help you maintain a clean atmosphere for your ritual work, as well as prepare you for the day when you will need to drive away an unwanted entity.

CHAPTER XIV

Grimoire of the Thorn

When I wrote the first edition of this book, I immediately began contemplating a sister volume, a spiritual sequel as it were. This book would have been a full grimoire, building on the principles established in the original work. However, aside from gathering the spirits and protocols required to work with them, that volume never fully manifested. Now, with the opportunity presented in this second edition, I want to include that volume here for those interested in working with these unique spirits.

Called the *Grimoire of the Thorn*, this text was inspired by what a friend once called "walking the thorny path," an indication that the way of the left-hand path worker was never an easy one, surrounded as it was on all sides by opposition. That description made perfect sense for these spirits as well, for they were conjured specifically to overcome that opposition through mystical might. The spirits presented in this work began as isolated spirits, but through years of work have grown into something more, to the point that they are ready to be called forth by anyone with the tools and the will.

Building upon what we have covered in previous pages, these spirits may be evoked, invoked, summoned for forging pacts and practicing possession, and can provide familiars to the sorcerer. Instructions for the necessary ritual structure and incantations will follow, and we will end this chapter with an introduction to each of the ten spirits of the *Grimoire of the Thorn*. You will find presented here a celestial and an internal authoritative spirit, as well as a pair of spirits for each leg of the crossroads: Love, Luck, Life, and Death. One spirit will act as the positive influence, attracting the more beneficial aspects of these things, while one will act as the negative influence, banishing these same aspects. In this way, these beings can be seen as something similar to planetary intelligences and spirits, though this comparison is not entirely accurate. Instead, it would be closer to the truth to say that they are mirrors of each other, though the reflections maintain an individual personality and energy. In any case, let us dive forward with no further delay.

When I felt that the time had come to assemble this grimoire, I set aside some time to not be disturbed. I lit some sandalwood and rose incense, a relaxing and pleasing scent, dimmed the lights, and entered into meditation. When I was firmly rooted in the meditative state, I allowed my consciousness to drift, rising into astral projection and following the currents of the divine. I breathed a small prayer to the universal divine, asking to be shown what needs I could fulfill through this working, and I was brought back to my first lessons in the art of hoodoo. I was taught that there is a crossroads with four legs, upon which hinges all acts of magick. These are Love, Luck, Life, and Death. On the road of love, we find all matters of relationships, romantic or platonic. This includes the forming, mending, and destruction of such things. The road of luck takes us into the gathering of wealth, as well as general good fortune. The life path deals with health and good living. And the death path deals with bindings, endings, and banishment in general. To these, I added another road, what I call the crux of the crossroads. On this crux, we have general magick, such as self-empowerment, spiritual authority, and other things that do not fall easily into the other four roads.

Upon seeing this, I then sought out through the divine the spirits of these roads, as well as the methods through which they may be contacted and worked with. I was then shown the ritual circle, illustrated below. I was told that a point of manifestation, like the triangle, was not truly necessary, but if the sorcerer so wished, a hexagram could be drawn outside of the circle, in which would sit a crystal, mirror, or other speculum for the spirit to manifest within.

I was then told that these spirits came in two facets, as mentioned previously. These would be referred to as the celestial and infernal facets. If the infernal facet was being called upon, one would set black candles at each quarter, upon the outer points of the dia-monds in the circle. If the celestial aspect was chosen, the candles would be white. The ritual circle was to be filled with incense smoke crafted for each spirit. It was to be a base of a tablespoon each of frankincense, myrrh, and white copal, along with a teaspoon of the corresponding herbs to each spirit, given below. The sorcerer would also add into the incense mixture the powdered ash of the seal of the spirit in question, having been burnt and powdered previously. The same sigil would be drawn out and placed in the center of the circle, or else under the chosen speculum within the hexagram. Finally, the sorcerer would need only a wand to perform the conjurations. There would be no need for an athame for the same reason that the hexagram was ultimately unnecessary: because these spirits pose no danger to the sorcerer.

Having made all these preparations, the ritual can begin. Light the candles and the incense, and allow the incense to fill the space while you meditate upon the spirit you wish to conjure and the goal for which it is being called. When the time is right, begin the opening litany. The opening litany is the invocation of authority that gives you the right to have communion with these spirits in the first place. When the opening litany has been recited, you will then give the first conjuration. This incantation opens the door between your circle and the ether, allowing the spirit to hear your call. The first conjuration is to be repeated three times. Then, the second conjuration is recited and offerings are given. This calls the spirit and entices them to appear, and should only be needed once, but can be repeated as often as necessary to establish solid contact. After this, you may commence with whatever work you have planned. When this work has been completed, you will give the dismissal. The dismissal should only be required once, but feel free to repeat if you deem it appropriate. Once the dismissal is given, the working is complete, and the ritual may be considered over.

Once you have made successful contact with these spirits through this method, you can begin communicating with them about potentially more streamlined methods, altering the ritual as it fits and as they allow, but initially, stick with the formula as given. It is not overly complex, and will provide a very direct conduit for these spirits to come to you.

The opening litany:

By the light that flows from the universal divine!
By the darkness that lives in its shadow!
Let all creatures of the heavens and hells,
all beings that walk the world, and all manner of entities,
seen and unseen, hear me and know my voice!
In this time that is out of time, in this space that is out of space,
let my voice be as the voice of creation!
Let my words now echo with the vibrations of life itself
and let all who hear them submit and obey!

The first conjuration:

I cast open the door between this world and the next,
and I make my circle the passageway through it!
By my will, let only those who have my
invitation in this hour come through,
and let all others stand aside,
for this is the will of the divine essence!
In this time that is out of time,
in this space that is out of space,
let this circle be the meeting point of powers,
that we may inflict our will upon the reality outside as we see fit!
Let all who have ears hear the divine edict,
and let them rejoice for my will is done!

The second conjuration:

(Name of spirit), I call to you!
Hear my voice, (name of spirit)!
(Name of spirit), three times now have I summoned you!
By the power of the divine light and shadow,

I conjure you into this space!
See the offerings I have laid before you,
and may they satisfy your hunger!
Bring to bear your power, your wisdom,
and your grace to manifest my will on this plane!
(Name of spirit), fill this circle with your force and flame,
that all that is not in accordance with my
will be consumed and cleared away!
Come forth, and make yourself known!

The dismissal:

(Name of spirit),
The time of our communion is drawing to an end.
May what has transpired here by inscribed upon
the stones upon which the universe rests,
and may my will be carried out!
Go now, and let us remain forever allies in the great work!

The next part of this chapter is devoted to meeting the spirits. These sections will contain the name and seal of the spirit, a description of their appearance and abilities, and a list of correspondences and offerings you can use to work with them. You may find things pleasing to them that are not on this list, and if so, you are advised to make a note of them for your own purposes. In any event, I hope that you have as much success with these beings as I have, and that you find them as pleasant to commune with as I do.

CALANTHUS

The first of the spirits I met, Calanthus, is the celestial aspect of the divine light. He comes in the shape of a young man with tan skin, green eyes, and white hair, swathed in robes of silver light. His domain is that of commanding spirits of the light, imparting divine wisdom, attaining psychic gifts, and exploring the akashic records.

Offerings: white candles, floral incense, clear quartz
Herbs: sandalwood, allspice, any mint

BARON LA'SON

The baron came to me on the scent of blood and fire, manifesting as the infernal darkness. A tall, dark man, dressed in a cape and suit so black that it appears to be shadow wrapping around him, his burning orange eyes see all. He rules over curses of all kinds, communication with the dead, and uncovering humankind's darkest secrets.

Offerings: black candles, blades, rotten wood
Herbs: dragon's blood, black cohosh, wormwood

KORICAPRA

Representing the beneficial aspect of the road of love, Koricapra appears as a woman with pale skin, pink hair, and blue eyes, wearing what could best be called dancing garments made of red and orange. She is called upon to draw love, generate charisma, and repair relationships that have suffered harm.

Offerings: perfume, jewelry, flowers
Herbs: catnip, roses, carnations

OCHOFAIRE

The detrimental aspect of the road of love, Ochofaire comes as a thin, bony man dressed in a slick violet suit, with a blackened rose pinned to his lapel. He carries in his hand a number of envelopes that he claims contain the secret shames of all men, and which he says he uses in his work. He is called to destroy friendships and relationships, to separate lovers, and to cause strife.

Offerings: chains, pins, stale cake
Herbs: galangal, High John the Conqueror, alum

CHILOPELMA

Appearing as a young, dark-skinned woman with light blue eyes and a white suit, Chilopelma carries a briefcase full of ledgers and tools to straighten out finances as the beneficial aspect of the road of luck. She speaks in a soft whisper that commands attention, and is stern but still gentle. She rules over gaining wealth and material goods, protecting what assets one already possesses, improving businesses and starting business ventures, and general good fortune.

Offerings: coins, gemstones of value, anything yellow
Herbs: calendula, cloves, cinnamon

LITODES

A tan man dressed in an orange robe, his features are concealed, but his meaning is clear. He is the detrimental aspect of luck, and he is the essence of greed. He can be summoned to take everything from a target, their wealth, their property, their business, even their good name. But he can also be called for positive things, such as to stop the loss of money in bad investments or poor spending habits.

Offerings: cooked meat of any kind, metal (especially iron), locks
Herbs: jasmine, vervain, cedar

AKHAFELIS

Akhafelis shows himself as an older man wrapped in the white coat of a doctor and carrying a Victorian-era medical bag, which serves him well as the beneficial aspect of the road of life. Under his authority are workings of healing, maintaining health, and keeping up with good habits such as exercise and proper diet.

Offerings: bottles, fresh water, vegetables
Herbs: eucalyptus, lavender, geranium

TATURA

Appearing as a skeletal figure in tattered clothes, Tatura's gender is impossible to determine. Even its voice sounds like a multitude of whispers speaking together. As the detrimental aspect of life, Tatura acts as a reaper, causing health problems, bringing harm, and even causing death.

Offerings: bones, hair, white wine
Herbs: dragon's blood, black pepper, saffron

CLEPHRIUS

Though she is the beneficial aspect of Death, Clephrius bears quite a pleasant appearance. Dressed in a pale green dress, she has fair skin, dark hair, and golden eyes. In her domain, we find the ability to end bad habits, as well as to remove that which we do not need. She can also be worked with for baneful workings, to bring the influence of death onto someone.

Offerings: flowers, amethyst, rum
Herbs: cinquefoil, Spanish moss, yew

OTANIAS

A wisp at the corner of your eye, a rattle of chains, Otanias does not like to take a perceived form, but when he does, it is as a shade of a man. His power lies in bringing negative things, bad habits, and cycles of misfortune into the lives of those he sets his sights on. His presence is often only known by the rattling of chains and the echo of ghostly laughter.

Offerings: chains, cords, grave dirt
Herbs: knotweed, elderberry, mugwort

Practical Work

Prepare your ritual area and summon one of these spirits to begin a relationship. It is best to begin with Calanthus, but you may work with them as you see fit.

PARTING WORDS

Well, it has been a long journey from the introduction to this point. We have covered several topics, and explored the depths of the spirit world. And what's more, if you have applied this work as you have read, then you have learned many valuable principles of the great work. My only hope is that you apply them well, and use my knowledge to further your own path, and the art in general.

One thing that I feel is worth mentioning is, no matter how advanced you are, you should never think you've grown behind the basics. While it is possible to become comfortable enough with your spirits that you can take some shortcuts, you should never neglect your foundation entirely. For instance, I've made many offerings to the guardian of my local cemetery, to the point that I can now walk through the gates unhindered, even without an offering. But I never neglect to leave one for the dead if I take something. It is a fine line, and only you can know where it is, but it should always be your goal to know where you are in regard to it. May the spirits watch over you, guide you, and bless you.

-Naag Loki Shivanath

GLOSSARY OF TERMS

Altar – A surface, usually a shelf or table, which holds the tools of magick and is typically the central point of ritual work

Animism – The belief that all things have a spirit of some kind

Artificial spirit – A spirit created by the magician; See also: Created spirit, Servitor, Thoughtform

Astral projection – The spiritual practice of inducing an out-of-body experience to allow the consciousness to explore the subtle realms

Athame – A ritual knife, usually wielded in ritual as an elemental representation of air, or as an instrument of authority

Banishing – Sending away a troublesome spirit from a person or place, typically through the use of spiritual authority; See also: Exorcism

Ceremony – A highly structured act of magick; See also: Ritual

Clairalience – The psychic sense of smell

Clairaudience – The psychic sense of hearing

Clairgustance – The psychic sense of taste

Clairsentience – The psychic sense of feeling

Clairvoyance – The psychic sense of sight

Cleansing – Purifying a person, place, or thing to remove negativity and spiritual attachments

Cold spirit – A spirit that typically acts slower, but more for the overall benefit of the magician

Consecration – A ritual that magickally blesses an item and imbues it with a purpose; See also: Dedication

Created spirit – A spirit created by the magician; See also: Artificial spirit, Servitor, Thoughtform

Dark spirit – A spirit that is typically more aggressive, stern, and prone to acts of wrath and violence

Dedication – A ritual that magickally blesses an item and imbues it with a purpose; See also: Consecration

Direct work – Magick that does not typically rely on spirits, instead making use of talismans, oils, herbs, and so on.

Evocation – A ritual that commands a spirit to come forth and commune with the magician outside of their body

Exorcism – Sending away a troublesome spirit from a person or place, typically through the use of spiritual authority; See also: Banishing

Familiar spirit – A spirit that serves the magician and is capable of carrying out a wide variety of tasks on their behalf, typically given to the magician by outside powers

Form sharing – A mystical technique that allows the magician and familiar spirit to merge into a single astral form to explore the subtle realms

Global spirit – A spirit that can easily manifest in multiple places at once and is not tied to a single point in space/time

Greater spirit – A spirit that is "higher up the food chain" so to speak, such as a deity, archangel, archdemon, and so on.

Hot spirit – A spirit that typically acts faster, caring about the result more than the general well-being of the magician

Immersion phase – A period of time in which the magician completely surrounds themselves with imagery and energy relating to a spirit for the purpose of building a solid bond

Incantation – A spell, chant, or litany that is recited with the intention of manifesting a result

Initiatory tradition – Traditions that are accessible only by being initiated by a priest, typically secretive and mysterious

Invocation – A ritual that requests that a spirit enter the magician's body and commune with and work with them from within

Isolated spirit – A spirit that can only be in one point in space/time at a time, typically tied to a specific place

Lesser spirit – A spirit that is "lower on the food chain" such as an elemental, servitor, and so on

Light spirit – A spirit that is typically calmer, more benevolent, and generally peaceful

Magician – One who applies his will, intent, and energy to the universe to create change in accordance with his will; See also: Practitioner, Sorcerer

Magick – The art and science of affecting change in the universe in accordance with the will of the one affecting the changes; See also: Sorcery

Offering – Gifts, such as food, fumigation, and libation, which are given to spirits in ritual to entice them to assist the magician

Pact – A bargain with the spirit to receive something in exchange for something else

Practitioner – One who applies his will, intent, and energy to the universe to create change in accordance with his will; See also: Magician, Sorcerer

Ritual – A highly structured act of magick; See also: Ceremony

Seal – A symbol that is intimately connected to a particular spirit or enchantment; See also: Sigil

Servitor – A spirit created by the magician; See also: Artificial spirit, Created spirit, Thoughtform

Sigil – A symbol that is intimately connected to a particular spirit or enchantment; See also: Seal

Sorcerer – One who applies his will, intent, and energy to the universe to create change in accordance with his will; See also: Magician, Practitioner

Sorcery – The art and science of affecting change in the universe in accordance with the will of the one affecting the changes; See also: Magick

Spirit house – A specially designed vessel that acts as a direct point of contact between a spirit and a magician

Spirit keeping – The practice of keeping spirits, usually lesser spirits, as companions for various purposes, such as protection, intelligence gathering, wealth attraction, and companionship

Spirit senses – Psychic correspondents to the five physical senses that are used to perceive and interact with the spirit world; See also: Clairalience, Clairaudience, Clairgustance, Clairsentience, Clairvoyance

Spirit work – Magick that relies primarily on assistance from the spirit world through evocation, invocation, and similar practices

Spiritual self-defense – Practices that make use of shields, rituals, and other techniques to ward off spiritual attacks and get rid of troublesome spirits

Temple – A space that is devoted to the practice of magick

Thoughtform – A spirit created by the magician; See also: Artificial spirit, Created spirit, Servitor

Thurible – A special type of incense burner that can be carried and used to move incense throughout a space easily

GLOSSARY OF SPIRITS

Aphrodite

Aphrodite is the Greek goddess of love, beauty, and pleasure. Born of sea foam, she had a hand in the legendary Trojan War when she chose to side with Paris and the Trojans. Aphrodite has a rich history, but her underlying theme is love, fertility, beauty, and grace. Aphrodite's colors can be said to be red, gold, and pink, and offerings to Aphrodite include red roses, apples, myrrh, pomegranates, and pearls.

Ares

Ares is one of the Olympic Greek gods, a son of Zeus and Hera. He is the god of war, and unrestrained conflict. He is the masculine energy of Mars that wipes away all opposition, leaving only cinders. His day is Tuesday, his planet is Mars, his color is red, and his incense is dragon's blood.

Azazel

Azazel is said to be the first archangel/archdemon who revealed himself to humankind, and taught them the way of war, beauty, and the occult. His secrets came from his being an angelic commander, close to YHVH, before his fall, and as his vengeance, he teaches men the way of the occult. His incense is dragon's blood, or a blend of mugwort and wormwood.

Barakiel

Barakiel is the angel of prosperity. He is first mentioned in the *Armadel of Solomon*, where he is said to hunt evil, and rule lightning, as well as to rule the month of February. He helps improve your outlook and attract abundance. Barakiel also enjoys the forest. His preferred incenses are pine, cedar, and sandalwood.

Buer

According to the Goetia: He teaches philosophy, both moral and natural, and the logic art, and also the virtues of all herbs and plants. He healeth all distempers in man, and giveth good familiars. His day is Wednesday, his planet is Mercury, his color is orange, and his incense is storax.

Bune

From the Goetia, the twenty-sixth spirit is Bune (or Bim). He is a strong, great and mighty duke. He appeareth in the form of a dragon with three heads, one like a dog, one like a gryphon, and one like a man. He speaketh with a high and comely voice. He changeth the place of the dead, and causeth the spirits that be under him to gather together upon your sepulchres. He giveth riches unto a man, and maketh him wise and eloquent. He giveth true answers unto demands. And he governeth thirty legions of spirits. His seal is this, unto the which he oweth obedience. He hath another seal. All that said, whichever seal you choose, he will respond to. His day is Friday, his planet is Venus, his color is green, his metal is copper, and his incense is sandalwood.

Furfur

From the Goetia: The thirty-fourth spirit is Furfur. He is a great and mighty earl, appearing in the form of a hart with a fiery tail. He never speaketh truth unless he be compelled, or brought up within a triangle. Being therein, he will take upon himself the form of an angel. Being bidden, he speaketh with a hoarse voice. Also he will wittingly urge love between man and woman. He can raise lightnings and thunders, blasts, and great tempestuous storms. And he giveth true answers both of things secret and divine, if commanded. He ruleth over twenty-six legions of spirits. His day is Tuesday, his planet is Mars, his color is red, and his incense is dragon's blood.

Lakshmi
Lakshmi is the Hindu goddess of wealth, abundance, and prosperity. She is known to be quite beautiful, and to be very easy to work with. Her offerings are sandalwood, rose, lotus, and jasmine, and her mantra is Om Shring Shriye Namah.

Leraje
According to the Goetia: The fourteenth spirit is called Leraje (or Leraie). He is a marquis great in power, showing himself in the likeness of an archer clad in green, and carrying a bow and quiver. He causeth all great battles and contests; and maketh wounds to putrefy that are made with arrows by archers. This belongeth unto Sagittary. He governeth thirty legions of spirits. His day is Monday, his planet is the Moon, his color is violet, and his incense is jasmine.

Loki
Everyone knows Loki as the adopted brother of Thor, the trickster. But what not everyone may realize is that he is also the Norse master of magick and illusion. His days are Thursday and Friday, his colors are red, orange, black, blue, and purple, and his incense is a blend of cedar, cinnamon, clove, and dragon's blood.

Malphas

According to the Goetia: He can build houses and high towers, and can bring to thy knowledge enemies' desires and thoughts, and that which they have done. He giveth good familiars. If thou makest a sacrifice unto him he will receive it kindly and willingly, but he will deceive him—that doth it. His day is Wednesday, his planet is Mercury, his color is orange, and his incense is storax.

Odin

Odin is the allfather of the Norse pantheon, the ruler and seer of all. He is the great wandering wizard, who hung from a tree for nine days to gain the knowledge of the runes for magick. His day is Wednesday, and his incense is a blend of clove, cinnamon, and allspice.

Paimon

From the Goetia: The ninth spirit in this Order is Paimon, a great king, and very obedient unto LUCIFER. He appeareth in the form of a man sitting upon a dromedary with a crown most glorious upon his head. There goeth before him also a host of spirits, like men with trumpets and well sounding cymbals, and all other sorts of musical instruments. He hath a great voice, and roareth at his first coming, and his speech is such that the magician cannot well understand unless he can compel him. This spirit can teach all arts and sciences, and other secret things. He can discover unto thee what the earth is, and what holdeth it up in the waters; and what mind is, and where it is; or any other thing thou mayest desire to know. He giveth dignity, and confirmeth the same. He bindeth or maketh any person subject unto the magician if he so desire it. He giveth good familiars, and such as can teach all arts. He is to be observed toward the west. He is of the Order of Dominations [Dominions]. He hath under him two hundred legions of spirits, and part of them are of the Order of Angels, and the other part of potentates. Now if thou callest this spirit Paimon alone, thou must make him some offering; and there will attend him two kings called LABAL and ABALI, and also other spirits who be of the Order of Potentates in his host, and twenty-five legions. And those spirits that be subject unto them are not always with them unless the magician do compel them. His character is this that must be worn as a lamen before thee, and so on. His day is Sunday, his planet is the Sun, his color is yellow, and his incense is frankincense.

Raphael
Archangel Raphael is one of the four cardinal archangels, along with Michael, Gabriel, and Uriel. He is typically regarded as the healing archangel, as well as the restorer of love. Raphael works by first increasing the bond of love between you and the divine, and then by expanding that bond from you outward. His color is green, his day is Wednesday, and his preferred incense is a blend of cinnamon and clove.

Sitri
According to the Goetia, the twelfth spirit is Sitri. He is a great prince and appeareth at first with a leopard's head and the wings of a gryphon, but after the command of the Master of the Exorcism he putteth on human shape, and that very beautiful. He enflameth men with women's love, and women with men's love; and causeth them also to show themselves naked if it be desired. He governeth sixty legions of spirits. His seal is this, to be worn as a lamen before thee, and so on. His color is blue, his day is Thursday, his planet is Jupiter, and his incense is cedar. One way to guarantee his favor is

to cut a piece of tin into a hexagon, carve his seal into it, paint it blue, and burn cedar incense on it during an evocation to Sitri on Thursday.

Thoth

Thoth is the Egyptian god of writing, revelation, and magick. He is also the god of education and learning, he was self-created from the beginning of time along with Maat. He is the ultimate deity of occult wisdom and knowledge, and worth the time to work with. His days are Monday and Wednesday, his planets are the Moon and Mercury, his color is white, and his incense is copal, sandalwood, and cedar.

A practicing Necromancer of almost two decades, Naag Loki Shivanath has devoted his life to studying the occult arts and sharing them in a way that is both illuminating and easy to understand. Beginning at the age of 12, he began exploring Wicca, Asatru, and Druidry, but quickly found his calling in Necromancy. Pursuing the winding green thread of death, he has explored numerous traditions, including Tantra, Vodou, Slavic Paganism, and Hellenism, but his home practice is Necromancy expressed through Brazilian Quimbanda.

His earliest magickal influences came from the works of Scott Cunningham, Donald Tyson, and Konstantinos, but in later life, he is drawn more to the work of Crowley, Inominandum, John Michael Greer, and Nicholaj Frisvold. This wide variety of inspiration has led him to embrace a more direct method in his writing, preferring clear, concise instruction to fluff and filler. With a focus on left hand path workings and spirit based magick, his work focuses on getting results in the most streamlined manner possible through whichever resource is most suited to the task.

Today, he uses his knowledge and experience to guide others in their mystical paths, and offer assistance when it is needed. In his free time, he is either in the company of other like minded pagans, or wandering through a forest, by a river, or through the graveyard, learning what secrets can be taught from the Other World.

REFERENCES & SUGGESTED READING

I have outlined below the resources that I drew on to create this work. They are arranged alphabetically and I recommend studying these works after you have worked through this book. While many of the spirit conjuring techniques that I have presented here, as well as those presented by several other authors, tend to be based on much older practices, the aspiring spirit worker may find it interesting to see the different ways each author interprets these methods. For that reason alone I recommend studying as much as you can and letting the truth be discovered through your own practices.

Agrippa, Henry Cornelius. *The Three Books of Occult Philosophy*. Novatio: Norman Publishing, 2009

Agrippa, Heinrich. *The Fourth Book of Occult Philosophy*. Whitefish: Literary Licensing, LLC., 2014

Alford, Sir Clifford. <http://www.nakedshaman.net/>

Connolly, S. *The Complete Book of Demonolatry*. DB Publishing, 2015

Filan, Kenaz. *The New Orleans Voodoo Handbook*. Rochester: Destiny Books, 2011

Laval, Gilles de. *Sacerdotium Umbrae Mortis*. Netherlands: Aeon Sophia Press, 2014

Leitch, Aaron. *Secrets of the Magickal Grimoires*. Woodbury: Llewellyn Publications, 2005

Mazohir. "*The Lesser Banishing Ritual of the Pentagram*." Kheper. 16 October 2000. 10 May 2017. <http://www.kheper.net/topics/Hermeticism/LBR.htm>

McBride Jr., Charles Leroy. *Runic Magick*. CreateSpace Independent Publishing Platform, 2017

Miller, Jason. *The Sorcerer's Secrets*. See also: *Miller's One Year Sorcery Course*. Pompton Plains: Career Press, 2009

Opus, Frater Rufus. *The Modern Angelic Grimoire*. Frater Rufus Opus, 2007

Peterson, Joseph H. *Arbatel*. Lake Worth: Ibis, 2009

Peterson, Joseph H. *The Grimorium Verum*. CreateSpace Independent Publishing Platform, 2007

Peterson, Joseph H. *The Lesser Key of Solomon*. Newburyport: Weiser Books, 1999

Qayin, S. Ben. *The Book of Smokeless Fire*. Nephilim Press, 2014

Skinner, Dr. Stephen. *The Grimoire of St. Cyprian*. Woodbury: Llewellyn Publications, 2010

Skinner, Dr. Stephen and David Rankine. *The Veritable Key of Solomon*. Woodbury: Llewellyn Publications, 2008

Warnock, Christopher and John Michael Greer. *The Picatrix*. Lulu, 2011

Worms, Abraham Von. *The Book of Abramelin*. Lake Worth: Nicolas-Hays, Inc., 2006

Other Titles by Crossed Crow Books
Death's Head by Blake Malliway
Craft of the Hedge Witch by Geraldine Smythe

Forthcoming Titles from Crossed Crow Books
Travels Through Middle Earth by Alaric Albertsson
A Witch's Shadow Magick Compendium by Raven Digitalis
Witchcraft & the Shamanic Journey by Kenneth Johnson
Star Magic by Sandra Kynes
A Year of Ritual by Sandra Kynes
Be Careful What You Wish For by Laetitia Latham-Jones

For more information about our available and forthcoming
titles, visit our website at
www.crossedcrowbooks.com.